DUNGEON of DEATH

DUNGEON of DEATH

Chris Benoit
and the
Hart Family Curse

SCOTT KEITH

CITADEL PRESS
Kensington Publishing Corp.
www.kensingtonbooks.com

CITADEL PRESS BOOKS are published by

Kensington Publishing Corp.
850 Third Avenue
New York, NY 10022

All Kensington titles, imprints, and distributed lines are available at
special quantity discounts for bulk purchases for sales promotions,
premiums, fund-raising, educational, or institutional use. Special book
excerpts or customized printings can also be created to fit specific
needs. For details, write or phone the office of the Kensington special
sales manager: Kensington Publishing Corp., 850 Third Avenue, New
York, NY 10022, attn: Special Sales Department; phone 1-800-221-2647.

CITADEL PRESS and the Citadel logo are Reg. U.S. Pat. & TM Off.

First printing: November 2008

10 9 8 7 6 5 4 3 2

Printed in the United States of America

Library of Congress Control Number: 2008932717

ISBN 13: 978-0-8065-3068-0
ISBN 10: 0-8065-3068-5

Abandon hope, all ye who enter here.

—*The Divine Comedy* by Dante

Contents

Introduction

There's kind of a running joke on my blog, although it's less funny as time goes on. It goes like this: I leave the city, and people die. To date, the deaths of more than ten professional wrestlers, that I've kept track of, have coincided with my not being around my computer when they died. The joke, which some have attributed to a curse on my part, or maybe just bad luck, really isn't that funny and never was, but sometimes you just have to cope with things as best you can.

It started with the death of Eddie Guerrero in 2005. First, I have to take full responsibility for his death, at least in the metaphysical sense. The weekend he died, my wife and I were on vacation and attending the wedding of friends in another city. While browsing through a flea market, we picked up a jade Buddha because it was supposed to bring good fortune and health. Well, I guess you get what you pay for with Eastern religion, because almost immediately upon bringing the Buddha into the car on the drive home, we got a call from my wife's friend letting us know that her grandmother had passed away that day. Later in the week, my wife's grandfather also died. And my cell phone was hit with a series of text messages letting me know that the wrestling world had lost Eddie Guerrero the night before. Truly this was a Death Buddha, although I'm thinking that it was our own inexperience with the whole concept that triggered such a series of catastrophes. Leave Eastern philosophy to the professionals, I guess. The Buddha currently resides on our coffee table and hasn't killed anyone else that I'm aware of, although they can be sneaky and you have to watch them.

But I digress.

I think the worst of it came in June of 2007, when Shane Bower, aka Biff Wellington, passed away in his parents' home, without much fanfare. Drugs were confirmed later, but then that wasn't a huge shock given Bower's previous troubles with painkiller medications. Everyone thought that former friend and partner Chris Benoit would probably be upset about it. I was pretty sad about it myself, because I had met Bower on a couple of occasions and found him to be a genuinely nice guy (an anomaly in wrestling to be sure), which made it easier to be a fan of his, even in the later days of his career when no one else was a fan.

A couple of days after Bower's death, Chris Benoit was scheduled to wrestle in one of the featured matches of the WWE's *Vengeance: A Night of Champions* pay-per-view event, where he was scheduled to win the ECW World title in a match with CM Punk. The day before the show, word got out that Benoit would miss the show, although that fact wasn't announced to the live audience at *Vengeance* until the match happened. At that point midcarder Johnny Nitro took Benoit's place and nothing else was mentioned by the announcers. It was declared a "family emergency," which most people I talked with attributed to Benoit grieving over friend Bower, and no one really thought much of it. That is, until the next day.

My wife called me at work on Monday morning, letting me know that she had read Chris Benoit was dead. My first thought was that she had obviously confused him with Biff Wellington (Shane Bower), as I had told her the night before about my previous meetings with Wellington and how he had been Benoit's partner and friend. It was an easy mistake to make. Later in the day, however, more details started to emerge and it was obvious it was no mistake—especially with the added and rather horrifying addition of the death of Benoit's whole family. I mean, that had to be an accident, right? It was a new house, so wild theories about carbon monoxide poisoning, which jibed with stories of Benoit reporting that wife Nancy was sick and coughing up blood, circulated and seemed to settle things. For about five minutes, that is. Sadly, the real truth was about to come out and was worse than anyone could have possibly guessed or imagined.

DUNGEON of DEATH

THE LIFE OF CHRIS BENOIT

They always said that he would never be a star, but in the end he will be remembered as the most famous professional wrestler in history, although not for anything positive. They always said that he didn't have charisma, but his death drew the attention of media from all over the world and served as the ultimate "heel turn" in a business filled everyday with fake storyline twists.

The Chris Benoit I knew, who was the best wrestler in the world more often than not and never had a bad word to say about anyone, was a totally different person than the guy he'll be remembered as, and I guess that makes it easier to disconnect the two of them. I prefer to think of Benoit as two different people, one guy who lived from 1967 until 2007 and the other guy who was created in 2007 and met a vile end after doing horrible things to the people he loved. Personally, I think it was slightly easier to cope with the end because Benoit was obviously coming to the end of his run in the WWE by 2007, and we as fans were mentally prepping for him not to be around any longer.

Growing up in Western Canada as a wrestling fan, you couldn't help but get sucked into the world of Stampede Wrestling, and all the kids at school had their own favorites. Some liked the various Hart brothers, although by the time my fandom came into full swing most of them were gone and the territory was down to Bruce Hart and younger brother Owen Hart. I didn't see the fascination, but I cheered for Owen anyway because he was exciting to watch in the ring. Some years later, he became my second-favorite wrestler in the world to watch; at the peak of his career he was forced to perform a death-defying stunt, but he couldn't defy death as easily as he could defy gravity. Other friends of mine liked Brian Pillman, who was a teammate of the Harts and won over the Calgary faithful with his own high-flying moves and gritty underdog story. Some years later, those high-flying moves took a toll on his body and he took too many pills trying to delay the inevitable end of his career and died as a result. Still other friends longed for the return of the greatest tag team to ever pass through Stampede Wrestling—the British Bulldogs—but when they did return, it was a shell of what they used to be. Ultimately, they self-destructed just as surely as everyone else in wrestling seemed to. And when all his family had split apart or died, Stu Hart, the guy who had engineered the whole Hart family dynasty in the first place, watched his wife pass away and then lost all hope himself before dying of what many considered to be a broken heart as much as anything.

So it's the story of Chris Benoit, mostly, but if you look back at the lives that he touched and the people that influenced him, you could almost say that a curse hangs over the Hart family and the promotion they built from the ground up. It's also the story of those people and others that I cover whose dreams, like Stu Hart's, were crushed by the heartless machine of professional wrestling. But let's save the sadness for later, shall we? Like I said earlier, I prefer to remember the good person inside Benoit, not the bad one who came out later.

Born in Montreal on May 21, 1967, Benoit moved to Edmonton at a young age and, like many other young kids at that time, instantly became a fan of Stu Hart's Stampede Wrestling (or Klondike Wrestling as it was known back then) and specifically the Dynamite Kid. In fact, according to the Kid's autobiography, *Pure Dynamite*, Benoit actually met him when he was 12 years old and received a bemused endorsement for his future career path. Although he always held up the Kid as a standard, he easily topped and greatly improved on anything that the Kid ever accomplished in the business. He would never admit that, of course, because that was the kind of guy he was. Despite being small and young, he emerged from the Hart Dungeon at age 18 and almost immediately became a homegrown star, winning the International tag team titles with Ben Bassarab, a title that he would go on to hold four times (with Keith Hart, Lance Idol, and Biff Wellington) during his career in Stampede. As a side note, his tag team partners also met with pretty bad ends, as Bassarab ended up serving a prison sentence for dealing drugs, which ended his wrestling career; Lance Idol died of mysterious causes in the early '90s; and, of course, Biff Wellington died a few days before Benoit did. As of this writing, Keith Hart is still alive and healthy. Whew.

Chris Benoit also held the British Commonwealth Mid-Heavyweight title four times during his three-year run with the company, most notably during a period when he was trading the belt with Johnny Smith. That particular rivalry, which saw the formerly cleancut Smith turning on Benoit and going heel, actually set the stage for a later feud that featured Benoit and teammate Davey Boy Smith taking on his idol Dynamite Kid and Johnny Smith in a sort of "battle of the British Bulldogs." That feud was supposed to revive Stampede again at the end of its run. It didn't, but it's hard to blame Benoit for that. Although he was becoming highly respected by his peers even at a young age, Benoit was always overshadowed by the only person in the territory who was even more talented: Owen Hart.

To forge his own name, Benoit started touring Japan in 1987, originally under the name "Dynamite Chris" (which he hated) and later under a mask as the Pegasus Kid. Although he initially hated being low man on the totem pole again, he grew to love the country and built his career around trips there. To say Benoit took the Japanese by storm would be an understatement, as he was trained again in the New Japan rookie camp and was instantly treated like a star because of his resemblance to Japanese legend Dynamite Kid. I should also note that the New Japan camps had a brutal reputation, often working new recruits nearly to death and engaging in extremely strict discipline routines. This training of course bears no small resemblance to the same treatment that Benoit endured as part of Stu Hart's Dungeon and goes a long way toward showing why his personality may have been the way it was. While jumping back and forth between Japan and Calgary, and later Mexico, he was earning a reputation as one of the top young workers on the international scene. He won the first ever Super J Cup in 1994 by defeating Tiger Mask's protégé The Great Sasuke in the finals. That match was notable for not only being off-the-charts great, but for also being a blow-by-blow tribute to the matches between Dynamite Kid and Tiger Mask that defined the light heavyweight style in Japan years earlier.

But while the Japanese loved Benoit, American audiences were indifferent. With Stampede long dead by 1992 and Benoit trying to break into the North American market again, he was limited to try-outs and one-shot deals to get a foothold. It is little remembered that the WWF actually wanted to sign him after giving him a tryout match against Owen Hart of all people in 1993, but his Japan commitments prevented that from happening. WCW was easier to work with, in that regard, thanks to their deals with New Japan, and so Benoit appeared for them doing weird stuff like a four-star tag team match with old partner Biff Wellington against Brian Pillman & Jushin Liger, or a four-star singles match in the opening match of *SuperBrawl III* against 2 Cold Scorpio. Apparently, however, having great matches and a cult following of hardcore fans just wasn't enough to crack the elite ranks of WCW, where top-tier talent like the Shockmaster, the former Tugboat who debuted on live TV by tripping and falling through the wall of the set, or "Evad" Sullivan, whose imaginary rabbit friend was a better worker than he was, were pushed to the main event. However, while doing yet another oddball one-off show, an AAA-WCW collaboration called *When Worlds Collide* in 1994, Benoit finally earned enough attention to get a full-time gig in the U.S.

That gig was in upstart promotion ECW, as Paul Heyman was a smart judge of talent and knew that Benoit had a built-in following. In fact, both the NWA (which was largely a joke at that point) and ECW were bidding for Benoit's services, and Heyman stole him out from under the lame-duck NWA, along with Eddie Guerrero and Dean Malenko. Heyman's plan was to build the company around Benoit, and to that end he was made the number two guy under ECW champion Shane Douglas, as Douglas formed a team with Benoit and Malenko that became known as the Triple Threat. It was kind of a Four Horsemen for the Gen-X set, and it was during this period that Benoit earned his first gimmick the hard way. He was wrestling Sabu, who was known for taking crazy bumps, and Sabu decided to use a strange headfirst landing off a simple suplex, which resulted in Sabu breaking his neck. Heyman immediately put his marketing genius into action and dubbed Benoit "The Crippler," finally giving him a "hook" after years of only having great wrestling matches as a gimmick. And once he was a star for the fledgling ECW and had a gimmick ready-made, WCW came calling again before Heyman could build his company around Benoit. Plus Benoit couldn't get a work visa thanks to Heyman's lack of organization, so he couldn't come back to ECW if he wanted to. It is ironic, of course, that WCW stole Benoit, Guerrero, and Malenko out from under ECW and Paul Heyman complained loudly about it because Heyman had done exactly the same thing to the NWA in the first place! Chris debuted in the fall of 1995 as a full-timer for WCW, although he still occasionally jumped back to Japan and won the Super J tournament in 1994. When the Four Horsemen reformed for the millionth time in 1995 with his friend Brian Pillman as the third guy, Benoit was brought into the group as the fourth Horsemen, although he rarely did interviews. But it was with that group that the next phase of his life would begin.

The Horsemen were feuding with Kevin Sullivan, who was booking WCW at that point, and Kevin wanted to have a major feud with Benoit because the matches would be great and he'd look like a mil-

lion bucks while wrestling him. They had a classic, genre-defining
crazy brawl at *Great American Bash 96*, which was Benoit's first big
push and saw him pinning Sullivan after suplexing him off a table
on the top rope. I should also note that at one point they fought into
the women's bathroom, resulting in every brawl that WCW put on
after that having to do the same spot. It's one of the rare matches
I've given five stars, because it set the stage for every "hardcore"
match that came after it.

However, to continue the feud, they did an odd deal. Here's the
setup: Nancy "Woman" Sullivan was married to Kevin Sullivan in
real life, but her role on TV was valet to Ric Flair and the Horsemen. Everyone knew that Nancy was married to Kevin, so they started
taping vignettes whereby Benoit would be romancing Nancy, at which
point they admitted the Sullivans were really married. That's not
the weird part. The weird part is that Kevin was so obsessed with the
realism of the angle that he demanded that his wife accompany Benoit
on the road and backstage, just in case someone saw them and reported back to the Internet that they might be having an affair "for
real." Well, Kevin Sullivan proved to be too smart for his own good,
as Chris and Nancy really *were* having an affair, which made the feud
only that much hotter. Unfortunately, Kevin found out about it and
his marriage collapsed, at which point Benoit moved in with Kevin's
wife and things started getting bad for him in his business life.

First, the Four Horsemen fell apart due to an injury sustained by
Arn Anderson. Then Benoit got involved in a lengthy feud with the
debuting Raven and ended up losing the majority of the matches
against his flunkies to build up the big blowoff between them. The
matches they eventually had were great, but now Benoit was being
manipulated by politics where he hadn't been before. The Benoit-
Raven feud somehow turned into a Raven-DDP feud with Benoit
also involved, because DDP was smart enough to raise his stock by
having great matches with Benoit. However, Benoit was the guy who
always ended up doing the job there (taking the loss to keep the

other two strong) and it left him almost totally directionless as a result, despite wrestling for the U.S. heavyweight title on a regular basis without ever winning it. However, by the midway point of 1998, WCW figured out that they could get another guy over by using Benoit, and booked a best-of-seven series between Booker T and Benoit to determine the number one contender for the TV title. This series quickly became the stuff of legend, drawing great ratings for Nitro and newbie show Thunder, and Benoit's fortunes appeared to be rising. However, he lost the series in the end and still had no titles to show for his years of service.

The problem was politics, in that WCW was a very political place and Benoit was not involved. Once he stole Kevin Sullivan's wife there was little chance of fair treatment, and he didn't have powerful enough friends to stand up for him. Things got worse when Kevin Nash took over booking in late 1998 and immediately put the WCW World title on himself and sent the promotion into a downward spiral from which it never recovered. Nash's feelings about Benoit and his smaller friends were well known, as he was quoted in one backstage meeting as describing them as "vanilla midgets" who could never get over. However, Benoit finally got a major title, winning the WCW World tag team titles with long-time partner Dean Malenko as a part of the final failed iteration of the Four Horsemen. But he was clearly going nowhere as long as Kevin Nash was in charge. Nash was finally cut loose in August, and Benoit was given a push by the temporary committee in charge of the promotion, as he won the U.S. title from comedy act David Flair before dropping it to Sid Vicious in a ludicrously booked match at *Fall Brawl 99*. I say ludicrously because everyone knew going into the match that Sid would win the title, because Sid was getting a main event push and didn't need the title or the win. And the match was even worse than expected because of Sid again. Before the match, agents specifically told Sid that at one point Benoit was going to lock him into his finishing move, the Crippler Crossface. Sid would then escape, but at no point should he tap on the mat because that would indicate submission. And what did Sid do when Benoit grabbed his hold at the crucial point in the match? He tapped the mat like crazy.

Benoit's highest-profile match came because of a sad circumstance—the death of Owen Hart. With Bret off for months to grieve and recover, the new management wanted to do a big match to pay tribute to Owen while they were running Nitro in the arena that he had died in. The natural matchup was Bret Hart v. Chris Benoit and the result was a modern classic. It was the longest match in the history of the program at nearly thirty minutes and an easy five-star classic that was carried by Benoit. Fan sentiment on who should have won was sharply split, with many (myself included) thinking that this was Bret's big chance to make Benoit into a giant star in Owen's name, but it wasn't to be, despite Bret's best efforts. The front office just had no interest in making him into a star . . . until Vince Russo came along.

At this point Benoit was booked as a part of a strange group called "The Revolution," a stable molded in the image of the Four Horsemen, with guys who were supposed to be angry about being held down by the old generation and stood up to do something about it. It consisted of the old ECW Triple Threat of Shane Douglas, Chris Benoit, and Dean Malenko, plus Perry Saturn added as a fourth. The funny thing is that everyone in the group really was getting sick of their treatment in WCW, and although they were "pushed" with token wins like Benoit's U.S. title reign, clearly the office had no use for them and were determined to "prove" that they weren't over enough to justify spending more time on.

Vince Russo's new regime changed all that because he's always loved the "young punks rising up against the establishment" theme, and he really loved Benoit. He immediately pushed Benoit as a top star of the promotion, and sent him all the way to the finals of a tournament for the WCW World title, but there were just too many flaws to overcome. First of all, Russo's booking is notorious for endless run-ins and storyline twists that are forgotten the next week, all of which rendered Benoit's in-ring storytelling an academic point. No one cared about any of the wrestling and Benoit had nothing to work with. Second, the tournament itself was a freakshow that featured thirty-two people in a promotion that could barely find screen time for more than twelve, and included managers and endless stipulation and comedy matches that killed any sense of drama the tournament might have had. Russo was clearly trying to replicate his greatest success in the WWF, the one-night *Survivor Series 98* tournament that made the Rock into the WWF champion and a main event star, but WCW didn't have the Rock, or Steve Austin, or a lot of guys who might have helped pull it off. Finally, with WCW dying faster by the day as 1999 drew to a close, Russo was out and Kevin Sullivan was rumored to be back in as booker, and Benoit had had enough.

Clearly with Sullivan back on top no one was going to get a fair deal and mutiny was the word of the day backstage. Wrestlers like to talk shit a lot, but this was serious stuff because Benoit knew that if he was stuck in the promotion any longer his career would be ruined, and it was time for a change. After lots of big talk, a huge group of wrestlers planned a walkout that turned into Benoit, Douglas, Malenko, Saturn, Eddie Guerrero, and Konnan. Things only got worse for the promotion as Bret Hart, who was scheduled to defend his WCW World title against Goldberg at January's *Souled Out 2000*, suffered a concussion. And then Goldberg decided to punch out a limousine window during a pre-taped vignette because he apparently thought that using his fist was just as good as using a piece of pipe, and he cut his forearm all to hell and couldn't wrestle. So they decided to run with Jeff Jarrett as champion, but then he suffered a concussion while wrestling three retired former stars in one night as a part of Russo's brilliant booking plans, and he couldn't take it. Even former UFC fighter Tank Abbott was pitched (which was what got Russo fired) and down the line went the title, like Judge Harry

Stone on *Night Court* getting his judge's job because no one else was home on a Sunday morning, being offered to guys who were smart enough not to want any part of it. Finally they essentially begged Benoit to take it, thinking that he cared enough about a belt to forget his threats, but to his credit Chris held his ground and said that if they put the title on him he'd throw it back at them and still leave. So they booked it anyway, a decent match where Benoit defeated Sid Vicious by submission (this time, Sid was *supposed* to tap the mat), and the next day Benoit was asked to stay after Sullivan was installed as the new booker. Benoit was never offered a chance to drop the title, and was so insulted by their treatment that he literally threw the title in the garbage can of the office and walked out with Saturn, Malenko, Guerrero, and Douglas. Konnan also tried to walk, but when the WWF didn't offer him or Douglas a deal they mysteriously walked back to WCW again.

Suddenly, Benoit was a hot commodity. The team that was immediately dubbed "The Radicalz" by the WWF marketing machine showed up on RAW in the front row and challenged top babyface stable D-Generation X on the spot. Of course, the honeymoon was short-lived, as D-X squashed them in a series of matches on Smackdown, culminating with World champion HHH beating Chris Benoit in Benoit's debut match for the company. Apparently Benoit needed to "learn how to work" all over again. This has long been a source of bitterness for me and many others, because Benoit was an international superstar before HHH even began his *training*. It looked like the same politics as in WCW, but in this case Benoit started having great matches with everyone and he was quickly pushed as a threat and people decided that after fifteen years in the business maybe he *did* know how to wrestle. He quickly got his first major title in the WWF into his run by winning the Intercontinental title from Kurt Angle at *Wrestlemania 2000* in a three-way match with Chris Jericho. He even got a shot at the main event at *Fully Loaded 2000* in July, facing the Rock in a hell of a good match where he appeared to win the WWF World title before the decision was reversed. Although he was drawing good numbers and having great matches, he always had the stigma of being WCW attached to him and was never able to break through. A brief feud with HHH at the end of 2000 produced another great match, but Benoit's reward was another trip to the midcard for the Intercontinental title instead of getting the big belt. Finally, in 2001, with the "Invasion" underway and former ECW owner Paul Heyman heavily influencing things, Benoit and Jericho were teamed up to win the tag team titles from Steve Austin and HHH, a match that was one of the best in RAW history and was intended to finally propel both guys to the main event for good. They followed up with a pair of singles matches pitting Benoit against Steve Austin for the World title on RAW and Smackdown, the latter of which was by far the greatest match in the history of that particular program and was taped in Benoit's hometown of Edmonton, Alberta. It almost succeeded in making them stars, but then HHH tore his quad muscle during the tag title match, derailing any Benoit v. HHH program right out of the gate, and the news got worse for Chris, even as the WCW invasion seemed to be tailor-made for him to break out as a star. Benoit was in another main event, a three-way against tag team champion partner Chris Jericho and WWF World champion Steve Austin at *King of the Ring 2001*, but Vince McMahon completely gave up on the match before the show started and booked a total squash by Austin, and he single-handedly beat the team who had been tag team champions just days before. Benoit still took a crazy bump on the back of his neck during the dead match, because that's what he did, but he suffered the consequences.

In June 2001, doctors informed Benoit that he needed neck fusion surgery after years of suplexes and diving headbutts, and he'd have to miss a year of action during the period when his career should have been taking off. He missed the entire WCW invasion (which some might argue was a good thing anyway) and returned to almost no fanfare a year later, and moved to Smackdown as tag team champions with Kurt Angle to build-up a main event feud between them. Again, Benoit wasn't going to win, but Paul Heyman was the guy in charge and pushed hard enough for him that they were able to do a strong match at *Royal Rumble 2003*; a match that drew Benoit a standing ovation. Clearly he was being positioned for bigger things, but the creative team changed again and Chris was out in the cold, stuck back in the tag team ranks and feuding with Rhyno in a pointless storyline that was leading nowhere for him. Oddly enough, at this point he was actually voted into the *Wrestling Observer* Hall of Fame for his years of great matches and technical expertise. I say oddly because he was still an active wrestler and also a guy who had never won a World title or been on top of a promotion before. However, he was voted in by his peers on the strengths of his work and being able to adjust to a multitude of different styles—everything from brawling to mat-wrestling to the vague "WWE Main Event Style" that dominated the new century. And for a while that seemed like it would be his biggest honor in the sport.

But by the fall of 2003, change was in the air. While I was chatting with a friend of mine on the writing team, he mentioned that they wanted to push Eddie Guerrero to the main event against Brock Lesnar, and they also "had plans" for Chris Benoit. Benoit quickly lost a great match to Smackdown World champion Brock Lesnar around that time, which I thought was the end of it, but little did we know that Lesnar was trying to get out of his WWE contract and they needed someone to carry the main event while they prepped newcomers Randy Orton and John Cena for the job. Benoit started feuding with Smackdown "general manager" Paul Heyman and the deal was that because he lost his title match, he'd never ever ever ever get another title match, unless he happened to win the Royal Rumble in January. And even then he was being forced to enter at number one, so you might as well just forget about it. And indeed, as was hinted by the setup, Benoit won the Rumble, going over sixty minutes and setting a longevity record in the process, thus earning a shot at the World championship of his choice at *Wrestlemania XX*. This, by the way, was clearly the greatest moment of my wrestling fandom, the kind of thing that we as Edmonton wrestling fans had been waiting for many years to witness: Chris Benoit being cleanly and definitively allowed to win the big match.

Then, at *Wrestlemania*, Benoit won the bigger match, making HHH submit to the crossface in a triple-threat match with Shawn Michaels also involved, and winning his first legitimate World singles title. Early in the build for the match it looked like a repeat of the DDP/Raven/Benoit debacle from WCW where a third person (Raven in that case, Shawn in this case) was inserted into a feud that was meant to get Benoit over, but the victory made it all the sweeter. It was a fantastic match, the best three-way match ever in my opinion, and ended the night in a sea of confetti with Benoit celebrating with fellow World champion Eddie Guerrero in a scene that will sadly never be seen on WWE programming again. Benoit defended the title in another great match at *Backlash* in his hometown of Edmonton in a rematch of the *Wrestlemania* main event. He actually went on to defeat HHH in subsequent rematches and, in the process, did something no one else in the sport outside of Batista can claim to have done: Definitively win a feud against HHH.

Sadly, if that was the climax of his career, the rest was the anticlimax. Benoit was told from the start that his reign would be a transitional one, because they wanted to pass the title to Randy Orton and, as promised, he lost the title cleanly to Orton at *Summerslam 2004* in yet another great match. The title didn't help Orton, who was a flop as champion. Benoit faded back into the midcard, having hit his peak and being satisfied with it. He moved back to Smackdown in 2005 and spent a good chunk of time as the U.S. champion, occasionally working great matches with new guys like MVP and Ken Kennedy and seemingly on the fast track for a career as head trainer whenever he decided that he had had enough of the business. By June 2007, the "draft lottery" sent him to loser brand ECW (once a fiercely independent promotion, now the dumping ground for the WWE's failed experiments) and he was scheduled to defeat hot newcomer CM Punk to win the ECW World title at *Vengeance 2007* and hopefully elevate him to the next level in the process.

On the night before the show, he called into the office to say that he wouldn't be there, and that's when the world fell apart.

THE DEATH OF CHRIS BENOIT

The dogs are in the enclosed pool area.
Garage side door is open.

—Chris Benoit's ominous text message
to co-workers and friends

I was working on Monday, June 26, 2007, when my wife called and told me that she had just heard that Chris Benoit was dead, along with his whole family. My immediate reaction was that she had confused him with former partner Biff Wellington, as I had been having a conversation with her the night before about Wellington's recent death and how Benoit had likely missed the PPV on Sunday night because of it. However, the sudden rash of text messages on my cell phone only confirmed the worst—it was indeed Chris who had died with his family, and the rumor was that everyone had suffered carbon monoxide poisoning in the new house. It was a horrible tragedy. Of course, it certainly turned out to be a tragedy, but not the kind we expected.

It is, of course, sad enough that wrestlers die on a constant basis. But sadder still is the fact that the WWE actually has a template to use for dead wrestlers. Indeed, that night was a Monday, so the normal Monday Night RAW telecast was cancelled and Vince McMahon sent everyone home, including the fans, so that they could air their usual Dead Wrestler Tribute Show. This tribute was actually karmic, creepy, and ironic on several levels, because the show they cancelled was a fake version of the Dead Wrestler Tribute Show. As a response to the outcry over the quiet ending to the long-running HBO juggernaut *The Sopranos* (which Vince had long thought of the WWE as being in competition with), the WWE decided to end the June 11 edition of RAW with a "bang," by having Vince's limo explode and the chairman be declared "dead" as a result. This would naturally lead to a big whodunit storyline where millions of fans would start watching the product again and no one would be at all offended or creeped out. I am, of course, being sarcastic here. Anyway, some people (myself included) had suggested politely that it was kind of iffy, karmicly speaking, to run a fake death storyline after basically ignoring the death of long-time WWE employee (and Hall of Fame member) Sherri Martell just a few weeks previously. In fact, the feeling from people who e-mailed me was "Boy, they'll sure feel stupid if someone actually dies while this storyline is going on." And so they did. But I digress.

It was the usual show that night as we all grieved and came to grips with Benoit's death. They re-played great matches from Benoit and wrestlers talked about what a great guy he was . . . and then new information started pouring out during the show. William Regal, who was one of Benoit's best friends and a guy who had his career revived by a match against him, merely noted that Benoit was a great wrestler and didn't add anything about him as a person. Then, abruptly, the tone of the show changed, going from a tribute to Benoit to a remembrance of his matches. Rumors that had been circulating about Nancy Benoit and their son Daniel vomiting blood started to change to stuff that was more sinister, and it was hard to come to grips with the ideas being presented by the press during the day. Even during the course of the show, the tone of the other wrestlers changed, as without fail they all noted how "quiet" and "private" he was. I was chatting about Benoit with people online, people who had been around or in the business for years and had seen everything already, and even they didn't know how to make sense of what was being said. Nancy dead by strangulation? Benoit dead by suicide? Benoit the only suspect in the double murder of his wife and son? Suddenly what had been a tragedy turned into a horror show, and my hero was rebranded into a modern version of Charles Manson. Information started flowing hot and heavy and each new e-mail I got over the course of the night was like another punch in the face. By the end of the day, there was a press conference with District Attorney Scott Ballard, who had been through the home in Fayetteville, Georgia, where the family was found. The home was declared "a major crime scene" by police and Ballard ominously said that "weird stuff" was going to come out of the investigation.

I thought that Owen Hart's death in 1999 was hard to deal with, but now I was being told that not only was Chris Benoit dead, but he was also a murderer and child killer as well. The natural reaction from fans was shock and denial, but the reaction from the WWE was even more pronounced and harsh. At the beginning of the ECW TV show the next night, Vince McMahon appeared and said "Last night on Monday Night RAW, the WWE presented a tribute show recognizing the career of Chris Benoit. However, 26 hours later, the facts of this horrific tragedy are now apparent. Therefore, other than my comments, there will be no mention of Mr. Benoit's name tonight. On the contrary, tonight's show will be dedicated to everyone who has been affected by this terrible incident." Although I'm sure everyone appreciated having a crappy third-string wrestling show dedicated to them, it was a nice gesture on their part and far classier than the tactics they used in the aftermath of Eddie Guerrero's death in 2005. The purging of the history records started in earnest, however, as Benoit's name was never to be mentioned again, he was purged from all future appearances on WWE 24/7, and all of his pictures and merchandise were removed from the WWE.com website. Although the WWE has the biggest library of wrestling history in existence, you don't want to get on their bad side. It was typical strategy from them, as they opted to pretend that this bad man didn't exist rather than face the problem. That being said, I'd have likely done the same thing in the short term to distance the company from Benoit's actions and keep the words "WWE Wrestling" from being associated with any mention of "murdering wrestler Chris Benoit."

So we know the facts, mostly. I don't think I necessarily need to rehash the gory details. But why would someone do what Benoit did? Medical reasons aside for the moment, it was a pretty stressful time in Benoit's life leading up to the murders. The death of his friend Mike "Johnny Grunge" Durham had hit him pretty hard, as had the death of best friend Eddie Guerrero, two of the people he depended on to keep him sane—so to speak. It's also apparent that the seemingly nonstop run of deaths of his former coworkers from Stampede was getting to him, as he had to watch friends like Brian Pillman and Owen Hart die young, or friends like Davey Boy Smith flush their lives down the toilet. The death of Stu Hart in 2003 hit everyone especially hard, because he was always the one constant in the crazy lives of Stampede wrestlers. Another factor may have been his failing marriage, as rumors originated with a friend of the family that Nancy maintained a safe deposit box with a letter in it essentially stating that if anything happened to her, Chris did it. Police never found anything in that safe deposit box, however. Whether or not it's true, just the fact that something like that would come out speaks volumes about the state of the marriage. After their deaths, it came out that Nancy actually filed for divorce in 2003 before reconciling with him shortly after. A few years before that, Benoit was arrested for a DUI, another fact that came out after his death in the media's attempt to somehow explain his actions by making him seem like a monster all along.

Really, though, the primary problem with sensationalistic media coverage of wrestling is that they fall prey to the same trap that they accuse fans of: They can't separate the character from the person. Although Chris Benoit played a violent sociopath in the ring, nothing could be further from the truth about him outside of the ring. Everyone who knew Benoit testified to his mild nature and family-oriented personality and, if anything, acting like a maniac in the ring probably helped him to blow off steam from his hectic real life. Which is not to say he was healthy. For Benoit, 2007 was a fairly dark time, as he was increasingly paranoid about his spot within the company and feared that ECW would be a step down and put his future in jeopardy. He was also starting to change his personality outside of his character by becoming far too much like the Stu Hart who tortured new recruits and expected the world of his sons. Chris's son Daniel was totally unlike his father, or any wrestler for that matter. He was a scrawny and physically weak young boy who would probably never be an athletic star. Just like Stu Hart and Fritz Von Erich before him, Benoit felt like it was his duty to push his son into wrestling and make him into his own image. In fact, he took a mentoring role with current young stars TJ Wilson and Harry Smith, and acted as a surrogate Stu Hart by pushing them to their limits like Stu used to do with him. Clearly Benoit was someone who wouldn't be able to deal with having his abilities in the ring limited by injuries and age, a situation that was rapidly approaching for him.

The weekend of Benoit's death reveals the depths of his illness and paranoia, as he exchanged phone calls with a WWE employee about missing shows that weekend and ended his phone call with "I love you," a bizarre thing to tell a secretary to be sure. By the time the scheduled *Vengeance* PPV would have started on Sunday without Benoit there, Nancy and Daniel would have already been dead. It was at this point that he gave the story about them vomiting blood, a story that spread to the messageboards online to explain his absence from the show. Benoit was actually scheduled to win the ECW World title at that show, although it's not known whether he was ever told that. Any speculation about the true motive is just speculation. We do know that Nancy was killed first, by strangulation with a cable cord, and Daniel was killed with a version of Benoit's crossface, followed by Chris hanging himself on a weight machine to end the weekend. The theories put forth by the police revolved around Chris losing custody of Daniel because the marriage was falling apart as a result of Chris becoming physically abusive to Nancy in his downward spiral after Eddie Guerrero's death, but this can't be substantiated by police reports. In the end, it wasn't the motives that captivated the media right afterward; it was the drugs.

Because Benoit left a virtual pharmacy in his house when he died and his initial blood tests showed elevated levels of testosterone, there was a spontaneous cry of "ROID RAGE!" in headlines around the country from people who had no clue what wrestlers did. It was the simplest and most believable theory for most—wrestlers take steroids, steroid users go into rages, end of story. However, the problems with that theory were immediately apparent to anyone who has actually followed wrestling for more than a month. Most wrestlers take levels of steroids equal to or greater than what Benoit was on but don't kill their families. And if they do experience so-called "roid rage," it's a short-term anger cycle where they do something productive like slapping an obnoxious fan at ringside or punching a hole through a wall of the dressing room. Killing your wife and son and placing Bibles by the bodies is not roid rage—it would be roid premeditation—and it totally goes against the kind of blind anger that steroids produce. The WWE quickly lashed out at the media for portraying the murders as a steroid issue, noting that there was no evidence of steroids in Benoit's body without an official toxicology report and that, in fact, Benoit had come up clean on his last steroid test in April 2007. However, to me, it just totally undermined their own drug program to come out and say that someone with literally thousands of pills in his house was not a drug user, when obviously he was. What does it say about the state of the Wellness Program when they couldn't even catch Benoit?

But it got worse. The next round of crazy media speculation centered around Daniel Benoit supposedly having "Fragile X Syndrome," a theory that even the WWE legal team endorsed as a rationalization as to why Benoit might have gone crazy and killed him. The speculation stemmed mainly from Daniel's small size and the fact that he was found to have human growth hormone in his system, which was administered by his parents. This was played up as another monstrous act, because what kind of sicko would shoot up his own seven-year-old son with steroids? Of course, no one actually wanted the answer to that question, which is "HGH was developed specifically for the purpose that it was being used on Daniel—to assist in normal growth in smaller children." The early talk show coverage was a circus, and the WWE declined to send anyone to shows that they perceived as not in the interest of the company (i.e., everyone but Larry King), and "reporters" like Nancy Grace and Geraldo Rivera brought bitter ex-wrestlers with axes to grind on their shows for maximum shock value. Not that the reporters didn't have a point most of the time, but in their rush to present the biggest story of the year (for that week) they actually let the WWE get off easy by reporting that twenty-seven wrestlers dying young in the past ten years was somehow a grossly huge statistic. In fact, the number is well over 100 wrestlers at last count and rising daily.* That would be a far bigger story if anyone would stop and ask tougher questions about it. We'll get into that can of worms in a little bit.

The drug angle would probably have faded away quickly with a combination of spin control and lack of interest from the public, but then we met Dr. Phil Astin as an offshoot of the investigations into the Benoit murders. The DEA, while looking into the horrendous amount of drugs found in the Benoit home, discovered that Benoit was using Astin as his "personal physician," much like the purpose that Dr. George Zahorian served with the WWF two decades previously. And like Zahorian, Astin prescribed huge amounts of painkillers and steroids to his clients, including a ten-month supply of what was believed to be testosterone cypionate every three to four

*Reported by the UK newspaper *The Sun*. The actual count was 109.

weeks to Chris Benoit. Although this was not linked directly to the murder case, police quickly took action against the doctor, casting an even greater shadow on the wrestling world as a result. The police raided Astin's home and indicted him on seven counts of distributing a controlled substance, with the initials "MJ" and "OG" coming up as the major names in the indictment. These initials were later revealed to stand for "Mark Jindrak" and "Oscar Gutierrez" (aka Rey Mysterio), thus making their Wellness Program even more of a joke. The search of Astin's records revealed that he had prescribed as many as one million dosages of painkillers and steroids, illegally undated, to various wrestlers and athletes. His records also indicated that Benoit's friend Mike Durham was among Astin's "patients," which set off a whole new round of media hysteria and talk show appearances for Durham's widow Penny, as they tried to tie the two cases together.

Toxicology reports didn't really tell us anything about the killings that we didn't already know—Benoit indeed had elevated levels of testosterone in his system, well past the limits established by the NFL and the WWE themselves, and Daniel was given Xanax to keep him calm (or even asleep) before he was killed. The tests couldn't say anything about the steroids or HGH present because there was no urine to test. However, once the fervor over the drug connection had died down, the efforts of former WWE wrestler and concussion expert Chris Nowinski came to the forefront. Nowinski, who is associated with the Sports Legacy Institute, had been campaigning to have Benoit's body examined for potential brain damage after years of taking unprotected blows to the head with chairs, as his mental breakdown mirrored that of similarly aged boxers and football players who had taken similar abuse to their heads. Normally, in wrestling, if you're going to get hit in the head with a chair, you put up your hands to cushion the blow. Benoit, a purist of the worst kind, insisted on taking them full force to increase the drama of the match. Even more physically damaging, Benoit would take his own moves full force. If you're not familiar with the way wrestling moves work, let me explain. When you jump off the top rope and headbutt some-one, the trick is to make sure your opponent not only doesn't get hurt but to make sure you don't get hurt either. Most wrestlers, if they're doing a diving headbutt, jump from the top and land on their knees well before they ever make contact, at which point they do a headbutt from that position. It's all so fast that it just looks like they're landing with their head. Benoit, because of his obsession with mak-ing it all look real, would absorb the impact with his head. You see now why this was so dumb for him to do. In fact, the first time he came back from neck surgery in 2002, even Dynamite Kid himself publicly asked Chris to stop doing the move, as did a parade of wrestlers in the WWE. Benoit even did simple things, like a suplex, where he would leave his own head unprotected and take the im-pact on his neck and head. In retrospect, I'm surprised he lasted as long as he did.

With the help of Michael Benoit, Chris's father, the body was re-leased to them and they found evidence of chronic traumatic en-cephalopathy, or CTE. This form of long-term damage to the brain had also been found in former NFL stars like Justin Strzelczyk, who also killed himself after a bout with depression in 2004. In fact, other symptoms like dementia and erratic behavior match up perfectly with what Benoit was going through. The findings of the Sports Legacy Institute (SLI) were that Benoit's brain was roughly equivalent to that of an 85-year-old man with Alzheimer's. According to the SLI, this brain impairment shows up primarily in boxers, with almost twenty percent of them suffering from it as a result of the repeated blows to the head that the sport produces. Jerry McDevitt and the WWE legal team were their usual sympathetic selves by issuing a reply to the SLI's findings that said "we're not going to dignify the crap they're peddling" and going on to note that many others have had concussions but didn't go out and kill their wife and son.

The WWE's handling of the situation notwithstanding, it does raise a lot of serious questions about the mental capacity of Chris Benoit leading up to the murders and how much of the blame can be laid on him. Certainly this is not to say that anyone else can be blamed for the murders except Chris Benoit. It was a horrifying act by someone who turned out to be a totally different person than the person we all thought that we knew, but could it have been prevented? We can never know the answers to why the murders happened, because everyone who was there is dead. I think this fact makes it more frustrating to try and put the killings into some kind of perspective that doesn't lead to Benoit being a psychotic killer who pissed away his entire life's work. He was having a bad year, personally, but none of his friends and co-workers, even those that knew him at home, would ever say that he was the type of person to commit such a terrible act of violence. William Regal noted in an interview with the *Daily Star* that he would "remember Chris for everything except the last two days of his life," which I think is the attitude that a lot of us are taking. As Dave Meltzer added in the July 2 *Wrestling Observer Newsletter*, "21 years is a long time to see someone start as a polite young kid, develop into one of the greatest wrestlers who ever lived, age rapidly before your eyes, and then completely lose his mind with little warning."

I think that although erasing Benoit from the WWE 24/7 library in the short term is a good move to distance the company from the murderer, in the long run it will be healthier for fans to remember the entertainer rather than the horrible person he became. The company line of the WWE following the tragedy was that they're in the entertainment business and, no matter the end that he met, Benoit was still one of the most entertaining wrestlers in the business. Wrestler Mark Kinghorn, who I talk with regularly, said it best when he told me "I'd maybe ask fans to remember Chris Benoit as the entertainer he was because that is the Chris Benoit we all knew and loved. Maybe I'd also tell them to be careful who they pick as a hero cause ya never know." I think that's the biggest lesson to take out of this, if there's anything positive to come out of it. Wrestlers and fans feed off each other in a weird symbiotic relationship; one side jumps off of cages onto flaming tables to draw a reaction and then blames their fans for pushing them too hard, while the other side puts their heroes on a pedestal and then acts shocked when they discover their action-figure physiques come from a bottle of pills. There has finally been some movement toward the positive with the implementation of the Wellness Program. Although many people (myself included) slag on it for being such a joke, at least it's something. Over the years the WWE has also toned down the crazy spots, to the point where Randy Orton's big spot is a headlock, in an effort to re-educate fans to storytelling without the constant use of ladder bumps and foreign objects.

It does raise an interesting question—do the deeds of the performer retroactively affect the quality of the performance? Someone noted on my blog that defending Benoit's in-ring work is like trying to separate Hitler the dictator from Hitler the painter. I don't think that's such a crazy notion, frankly. If you have moral high ground enough to judge the entire body of work of a man because of his deeds in real life, then bully for you. It must be nice to be so righteous. I think it's sad, and it's a tragedy, and Benoit proved to be a horrible human being who got exactly what he deserved, but in the end unless you were related to Nancy and Daniel it's hard to justify acting like you knew them any better than Benoit's long-time fans knew him. In the end, it will all be explained in a TV movie or on an episode of "Law & Order," and we'll all go on with our lives doing the best we can to cope or mourn or forget about it. I'm glad I didn't know Benoit the person, because it would have made it a lot tougher to like Benoit the performer. If nothing else positive can come out of this whole sick situation, it's that I can still enjoy his matches and hope that one small bit of happiness can overcome the crushing horror of those awful two days. I'll take what I can, I guess.

STU HART AND STAMPEDE WRESTLING

In his autobiography, *Hitman: My Real Life in the Cartoon World of Wrestling*, Bret Hart compared his father's beloved Stampede Wrestling to a "runaway locomotive," losing $5000 a week. You'd think that any sane businessman or father would want to keep his children as far away from that kind of proposition as he could, but that's not the lesson that the history of wrestling has taught us. In fact, it's quite the opposite. There is no denying the incredible influence that Stu Hart had on the sport of professional wrestling over the course of his life. All of the main players of this book can be traced back to Stu. And when it came to training, his hard-working attitude created the person that Chris Benoit became. Although he was never a top star in the wrestling business during his years as a worker or a top promoter when it came to drawing money, the waves of wrestlers he trained and influenced in his little promotion in Calgary have lasted years beyond the end of the promotion and even beyond his own life. That said, however, had many of the people he created not been brought into the business, they'd likely still be alive today—like Brian Pillman, Davey Boy Smith, and Junkyard Dog. Or still be happy and healthy, like Dynamite Kid, Superstar Billy Graham, and Jake Roberts. So influence and historical significance can certainly cut both ways.

The legend of Stu Hart began early in his life in the 1920s, when he witnessed a match with Canadian wrestler Jack Taylor and was determined to follow that life for himself. In becoming something of an amateur star early in his career, Hart used his training sessions to develop the brutal self-discipline and endless array of painful holds that would later instruct (and torment) generations of future wrestling stars and wannabes. He was a strict, clean-living health nut (in the days before that became a mainstream lifestyle choice) and maintained that stance all through his life. As a result, Hart became an amazing physical specimen and one of the greatest amateur wrestlers that Canada ever produced. Although he wasn't wealthy enough to pay his way to the Olympics, he tried to get sons Bret and Owen to follow his lost dream and pursue the goal he could never reach, which is one of the primary reasons why they were dragged into wrestling instead of being allowed to follow their own ambitions. Both Bret and Owen later came to love wrestling, but they have stated they would never have gotten involved in the sport had Stu not pushed them. Some would even argue that taking the boys into the basement and stretching them until they were howling and in tears of pain and terror was a form of child abuse, and a rather blatant one at that. Stu's basement in the Hart mansion, where such stretching occurred many times over the years, became known as the Hart Dungeon, and many people feared what would happen to them when they got there.

Stu wrestled professionally until 1960, and though he never won a major singles title he drew good money wherever he went, and began promoting his own wrestling company in Calgary. He quickly became known for taking in bodybuilders and football players and turning them into champion wrestlers. One of his first conquests was Archie Gouldie, who later became known as the Mongolian Stomper and gained worldwide fame, but nowhere more than in Calgary. Gouldie was an arrogant fan who decided to take matters into his own hands and attack some of the top heels one week, hoping to win himself a job. Stu took him into the Dungeon and gave him what many have related to be the worst beating he ever gave a man, stretching and humiliating him for hours until he begged for mercy and finally ran away in pain. However, Archie returned a few months later, politely asking to be trained to wrestle after apparently having learned his lesson. Stu had that effect on people, I guess.

Perhaps one of the biggest influences that Stu had on the business was taking bodybuilder Wayne Coleman and turning him into Superstar Billy Graham, who went on to become WWF World champion by beating Bruno Sammartino. But rather than the dubious fake achievements that Graham accumulated, it was his outlandish interview style and tie-dye wardrobe in an era where big hairy lugs with no charisma ruled the airwaves that really earned him a place in wrestling history, predating such future genre-defining wrestlers as Hulk Hogan and Scott Steiner. Graham was not only a bona fide superstar in the '70s, he was one of the guys who popularized the steroid lifestyle for wrestlers and acted as a distributor and teacher to an entire generation of wrestlers looking to enhance their natural attributes with drugs. Graham has since said that he has no regrets about his lifestyle choices, much like Dynamite Kid, even though the drugs destroyed his liver and eroded his bones to the point where he needed hip replacement surgery late in his career. Stu has long considered Graham his greatest accomplishment in terms of turning a nobody into a star.

The era of Stampede Wrestling officially began in 1967, after previous incarnations as Big Time Wrestling, Klondike Wrestling, and Wildcat Wrestling, although the promotion was never a huge success. Despite making money hand over fist in the '50s with older versions of the promotion, a remark made by Iron Mike Dibiase on TV in 1963 about how if brains were dynamite the people of Calgary couldn't blow their noses got them thrown off TV. Although it sounds pretty tame today compared to the filth aired by Vince McMahon on "family friendly" shows, it was way over the line for the time. Without TV, Stu struggled to keep the company afloat until the '70s, when former victim Archie "The Stomper" Gouldie returned to the territory and engaged Abdullah the Butcher in a series of horrifically violent matches that instantly brought Stampede Wrestling back from the dead. Fans in Calgary, who were hard-working miners and lumberjacks, paid money to see hard-working wrestlers put on no-nonsense shows filled with realistic matches, the way that Stu liked it himself, and the wrestlers were able to build their work around that attitude. Unfortunately, because brawls like those between Abdullah and Gouldie drew well, Stu took things too far and brought in "garbage" wrestlers Mark Lewin and Curtis Iaukea as headliners in 1975. Garbage wrestling offers no skill, it's merely tons of weapons and blood with no effort to duplicate the realism offered by someone like Gouldie, and the territory fell apart with them on top. Ed Whalen, the announcer and backbone of the show, quit during a TV taping, disgusted over the direction things were going in.

Things appeared hopeless for Stu's company at the end of the '70s, but with a new decade came the changes that would revolutionize his business and wrestling in general. And that was in the form of Tom "Dynamite Kid" Billington, a light-heavyweight from Britain who blew into Calgary like a hurricane. Ed Whalen returned to call the action again, and soon Stu had a group of his sons old enough to push as the new generation of stars against the evil Dynamite Kid. Soon the Kid's cousin, Davey Boy Smith, joined him and things changed forever. The change came not just because the future British Bulldogs were such great workers (although they were that), but also because the Kid was the hottest act in the territory and now they were building an entire company around guys who were traditionally not thought of as big enough to headline. And because Stu's own children were not giants themselves, he could push them to the top in legitimate main event contests against Dynamite Kid, and suddenly there was a whole new philosophy of wrestling ten years before Eric Bischoff claimed to have innovated the cruiser-weight division. Furthermore, Stampede picked up stars from around the world and integrated styles from Japan and Mexico into the standard North American one, and became a melting pot of wrestling goodness in one little city. It was this attitude that produced names like Bret Hart, The British Bulldogs, and, later, names like Brian Pillman, Owen Hart, and Chris Benoit. Years later Stampede became a breeding ground for young and hungry Japanese stars like Keichi Yamada (who was later turned into Jushin "Thunder" Liger and became an international superstar) and Hiroshi Hase (later a huge star in Japan, and a wrestler who actually became a successful politician, too!).

But the golden age had to end, and it was once again thanks to Bruce Hart's booking excesses. The company's biggest heel was clearly Allen Coage, who wrestled as Bad News Allen and later became more famous as Bad News Brown in the WWF. A former judo champion who began wrestling later in life, Bad News was legendary for his real-life fighting prowess, as well as being one of the few guys to ever talk down Andre the Giant. While waiting around on a tour bus during a stint with Stampede in the '70s, Andre apparently made a rather racist remark, not knowing that Allen was nearby. Bad News called out the Giant for his loose tongue, and Andre respectfully declined to leave his seat and answer that challenge, pretending not to have heard. It instantly cemented Allen as the toughest man alive in the minds of everyone there. Bad News is also a victim of the Stampede curse, having died in 2006 of a heart attack, albeit well over an age that it would be considered unnatural. Still, it sucked. Anyway, I digress. Bad News was the man in Stampede in the mid-'80s, dubbing himself the "Ultimate Warrior"—years before Jim Hellwig took that name for himself and went crazy—and he destroyed whatever hapless opponents were thrown his way. So naturally Stu had visions of the glory days of Stomper v. Abdullah when Archie Gouldie returned to the promotion and seemed like a natural to match up with his top heel. Bruce Hart crafted a face turn for the Stomper to set up the main event program for the summer: They brought in jobber Tommy Lane from the southern U.S. and changed his name to "Jeff Gouldie," with the gimmick being that he was Archie's rookie son who was trying his hand at the business so that his dad could retire and pass the torch to him. Lane eventually went on to some small amount of stardom as half of a team called the Rock N Roll RPMs with Mike Davis (who also died fairly recently of drug-related causes), but at that point he was an unknown. Bad News teamed with The Stomper and his "son" in a six-man match against the Harts, but then turned on his partners and injured Jeff so badly that he had to be taken to a local hospital, thus ending his career after the first match. Gouldie, after the match, gave what is without a doubt my favorite interview in the history of wrestling, when he expressed all his hurt and sorrow and rage in one five-minute rant and essentially threatened to kill Bad News Allen in several different ways for robbing his only son of the chance to carry on the family name.

However, the gimmick worked so well that fans literally rioted trying to go after Bad News and stop his attacks on Jeff Gouldie, and it was a disaster for Stampede in no uncertain terms. They got thrown off TV again, and Ed Whalen quit over the bloodshed again, and now there was no fighting off the advancing WWF. Stu sold the company to Vince McMahon in 1984 with a promise of $1,000,000 over ten years and a push for Stu's sons in the WWF. Although Vince was more than happy to push his new acquisitions in the form of the Hart Foundation and the British Bulldogs, he quickly reneged on the money owed to Stu and gave him his company back. It wasn't the first time he screwed over a member of the Hart family, of course. The doors reopened in October 1985 and they even got a TV deal with TSN, the new national sports network in Canada. The talent pool was propped up with incoming Japanese stars and the tremendous work of Owen Hart, but despite the buzz that this new incarnation was causing and the stars it was creating, they just couldn't compete with the WWF machine in the Western Canadian market. Vince snapped up whatever few stars they could create (Honky Tonk Man and Bad News Allen most notably), and even a strangely hot angle with former jobber Karl Moffat playing a serial killer named Jason the Terrible was not enough to maintain any kind of momentum. It should be noted, however, that the psychedelic green-screen promos with Jason and his manager Zodiac (played by Randy Orton's estranged uncle Barry Orton) were odd harbingers of the more eclectic interview style pioneered by ECW years later.

By 1989, everyone was gone and Stu made the mistake of putting the returning Dynamite Kid in charge of booking the company and that was enough to kill it for good. Times had changed too much and the hard-working company in Calgary couldn't change with them. It wasn't for lack of trying, because Bruce Hart for all his stupid ideas was a visionary booker who foresaw many of the changes that would reshape wrestling in the '90s. However, those ideas didn't make money in the '80s and that was the problem. In the end, Stu got what he really wanted: All his sons were wrestlers and all his daughters were married to wrestlers. Some, like Georgia, even produced wrestlers themselves, giving the world Teddy Hart. A second-generation Stampede has run shows in Alberta for the last few years, but like most endeavors that pay tribute to the original, it's never the same. Ed Whalen, the voice of Stampede Wrestling, died in December 2001, which robbed us of the heart and soul of the show. Stu's wife Helen also died in 2001, which drained Stu of any desire he might have had to continue with his passion. Stu himself died October 16, 2003 of pneumonia, but everyone who knew him said that it was as much from a broken heart as anything medical.

THE BRITISH BULLDOGS

Davey Boy Smith and Tom "Dynamite Kid" Billington both got their North American starts in the early '80s as a part of Stu Hart's Stampede Wrestling in Calgary. As with many teams widely recognized as being great, Davey Boy Smith and the Dynamite Kid started their tenure as bitter rivals—Dynamite the cocky heel and Davey Boy the sympathetic babyface.

Tom Billington, born and raised in the slums of England, got his start as a teenager in underground wrestling matches for small paydays. Dynamite was always very sure of his career as a wrestler, and it showed in his spectacular matches and willingness to take any risk to get over. After winning several mid-heavyweight titles in his home country, he met Bruce Hart in 1978 (on a tour of the country) and impressed him so much that Hart decided to recruit him for his father's Stampede Wrestling in Canada, long regarded as one of the highest-quality promotions in terms of "real" wrestling action that could be found in North America. The Kid spent five years there, amazing audiences with his suicidal bumps. Example: Bruce Hart is out on the concrete floor, and Dynamite comes off the top rope with a headbutt attempt that misses. He lands face-first on the concrete with no protection, then proceeds to repeat that same spot night after night on a tour of small towns in Alberta. The one thing considered to be holding the Kid back was his lack of size, which he unfortunately attempted to compensate for by bulking up with anabolic steroids. As Billington noted in his autobiography:

I'll be honest, I was into serious stuff with the steroids. I was taking at least 6 CCs of testosterone—3 CCs in each arse cheek—every day, which could make you feel very bad. And I went from about 180lbs to 225lbs.

He also began using drugs regularly to ease the pain that his bumping caused him. Although it temporarily allowed him to continue his high-energy style in the short term, later on it would cost him.

The Kid departed for a tour of Japan in 1979, and soon began a series of matches in New Japan with another up-and-coming superstar: Satoru Sayama, who wrestled as the first Tiger Mask. The Kid and Tiger Mask thrilled audiences with their matches over the NJPW junior heavyweight title in that period, until finally Dynamite returned to Stampede with a new international reputation. Along for the ride came Davey Boy Smith in 1982. Billington's younger cousin (born November 1962) and another British import for Stampede, Smith, who was less of a sensation than the Kid, chose a more conservative style within the light-heavyweight division. Soon the two men matched up as bitter enemies, with Dynamite playing the heel. This proved to be successful enough in elevating Dynamite (in addition to his rapidly increasing size) that he was given a run as North American champion before beginning a team with Davey Boy Smith.

When Stampede Wrestling was sold to Vince McMahon in 1984, part of the deal was that Vince would "take care of" Smith, Dynamite, Bret Hart, and Jim Neidhart. However, Smith & Dynamite were making far more money working for Shohei Baba in All Japan than they were doing spot shows for the WWF at $500 a night. Even more importantly, their escalating size due to steroids got young Japanese fans excited to see them matched up against traditional monsters like Stan Hansen and the Funk brothers. More often than not, the cousins teamed up in Japan and made $6,200 a week in the process and turned themselves into a hot commodity in the U.S. After initially letting them quit to work Japan, Vince signed them back for bigger money and struck a deal with Baba that would allow him exclusive use of the newly named British Bulldogs.

Just like in Japan, the Bulldogs were instant sensations in the WWF by blending their new power repertoire with the high-flying moves that had made them stars in the first place. For example: While wrestling jobbers, Smith powerslams one of them, then puts another over his shoulders. Meanwhile, the Kid climbs to the top rope, jumps onto the poor guy still sitting on Smith's shoulders, and from that position hits a diving headbutt into the guy who just got power-slammed. The crowds would go nuts to see stuff like this, and the Bulldogs obliged by doing more and more of it every night, all the while not needing to cut a single interview. However, even at the top of the tag team world this early point in their career, injuries were piling up. Dynamite had long been using painkillers to deal with his back injuries and Davey Boy soon followed suit, although he didn't go public with the kind of excruciating pain he was dealing with until well after his career was over.

Dynamite Kid raised some eyebrows by being booked in the Wrestling Classic tournament and doing three matches in one night, going over Nikolai Volkoff and Adrian Adonis before bowing out to Randy Savage in the semi-finals. Davey Boy was also entered and did an injury angle in the first round to explain his early exit to Ricky Steamboat.

After disposing of early rivals in the Hart Foundation (fellow Stampede alumni Bret Hart and Jim Neidhart), the Bulldogs were given a title shot at the tag champs, Greg Valentine & Brutus Beefcake. Despite Valentine's best efforts to carry the team on his back, it was mainly a star vehicle for Hogan's friend Beefcake and the match quality suffered as a result. The Bulldogs gave them not only some much-needed hot matches to wow the crowd but, more importantly, credibility as champions, which was something that had been missing. The Bulldogs began a lengthy chase of the tag titles as the fans simply wouldn't write them off as contenders and demanded more shots at the titles for the increasingly popular team. Finally, figuring that more money could be made with the Bulldogs as champions than not, the WWF gave the Bulldogs a manager in Captain Lou Albano to cut promos for them, and put them over Valentine & Beefcake for the titles at Wrestlemania 2 in what was generally considered the best match of the show. The match was well worked on both ends, but the finish was typical Dynamite craziness. He stood on the top rope and allowed Davey to ram Greg Valentine's head into his own and took a flat back bump to the floor in the process. Luckily, the match was a ★★★½ affair. To give the team an additional bit of star power, rocker Ozzy Osbourne was in their corner, which produced the rather surreal sight of Ozzy and Lou Albano celebrating with the tag belts while Dynamite laid on the floor, probably requiring medical attention. Sadly, this match would prove to be the Bulldogs' peak in the WWF as a team.

The Bulldogs held the tag titles for nine months, a very healthy reign, and spent the majority of the time defending against old rivals like the Hart Foundation and the Dream Team. However, tragedy struck as 1986 drew to a close: During a match with Magnificent Muraco & Bob Orton, the Kid attempted a hiptoss on Muraco, only to feel his back give way and the match was hastily ended so medical attention could be sought. The problem, it seemed, was that years of steroid abuse had deteriorated the Kid's back to the point he shouldn't have been able to walk. However, the other drugs that Kid took for everyday painkilling blocked the back problems so effectively that he was in traction by the time he realized the severity of them. Even worse, he attempted to continue working through the injury for a short time because job security is never assured in wrestling. As Kid explained in his autobiography:

> Your wage depended entirely on business, and on where you wrestled on the card. For example, if you were in the first

match on a spot show, you might get $200. Second match, you get $300, and so on, up to the main event, where you could get $2000. . . . But even that could change from one night to the next, so you never knew how much you were going to get paid.

The back injury suffered by Dynamite probably should have ended his career. Normally this would be followed by an inspirational comeback on his part where he returns better than ever, but when I say that it probably should have ended his career, I mean that literally. He suffered two ruptured discs in his back and also had partial paralysis from the nerve damage and was unable to get insurance because of his profession and reputation. Vince can be cold-hearted, but the situation was clear in this case: The belts needed to be changed and quickly.

The situation worked out somewhat well for the WWF, as the huge number of babyface teams working in the promotion at the time (Killer Bees, Can-Am Connection, and the Islanders, to name three) meant that a strong heel champion in the tag division was preferred. After weeks of no-shows on the Bulldogs' part, Vince decided to switch the tag titles to Iron Sheik & Nikolai Volkoff, but Kid was having none of that. If he was going to pull himself out of a wheelchair and get into the ring, he was only going to drop the titles to someone he respected. So in January 1987, Dynamite was literally dragged out of his hospital bed and ordered to defend the tag belts with Davey Boy against the Hart Foundation for a TV taping in Tampa, Florida. Dynamite couldn't walk, so Davey Boy piggybacked him on his shoulders to the ring and helped him to stand on the apron long enough for the heels to "knock him off" and allow him to rest on the floor. Davey Boy then wrestled the entire match alone and lost the titles, to the shock of the fans. The whole thing took ninety seconds total, if that. Dynamite was returned to the hospital, where the doctors informed him that he would never wrestle again.

But Dynamite Kid was nothing if not stubborn, and only two months later he was back, which was still months earlier than doctors recommended returning. After engaging the Hart Foundation in a memorable 2/3 falls rematch on an episode of SNME, a six-man was signed for Wrestlemania III with the Bulldogs and Tito Santana against the Hart Foundation and evil referee Danny Davis. The story with Davis was fairly straightforward: He was a middling wrestler who was forced by lack of talent to go into refereeing but still wanted to be a wrestler. So a storyline was created whereby Davis would start out with a bias toward heels, which led to him "screwing" the Bulldogs out of the tag titles in the title match by ignoring all the cheating of the Hart Foundation. Later, it was retroactively established that Davis had been biased when refereeing the match that put the Intercontinental title on Randy Savage, thus giving wronged ex-champion Tito Santana a reason to hate him. And make no mistake, Davis was amazingly over as a heel, capitalizing on the general hatred of a referee that any sports fan has. Added to this was Davis' arrogant smirk as he grew more and more evil. He was finally fired before a match on national TV and "suspended for life" from refereeing (life in this case being 1989), which gave him the loophole he needed to become a wrestler.

The six-man was, not surprisingly, a very good match, which featured Davis getting the living daylights beaten out of him by the Bulldogs and Santana before heel tactics on the part of the Harts allowed Davis to nail Davey Boy with manager Jimmy Hart's ever-present megaphone and get the upset pin. This match pretty much put the final touches on the Harts-Bulldogs feud, as Dynamite Kid took some much-needed time off before getting bored and re-forming the team in November. By this point, however, Dynamite was a one-dimensional worker, doing the occasional punches and kicks and headbutts but mostly standing on the apron and letting Smith do the bulk of the heavy lifting.

However, with Lou Albano having left the promotion and Dynamite Kid wrestling as a shadow of his former self, the WWF felt they needed something to distinguish them as a tag team. So they gave the Bulldogs . . . a bulldog named Mathilda. The WWF immediately went in the direction that everyone feared and had a heel team kidnap the "beloved" dog and the Bulldogs sought revenge. In this case, it was the newly heel Islanders who did the evil deed, and it led to a six-man match at Wrestlemania IV with the Bulldogs and Koko B. Ware taking on The Islanders and manager Bobby Heenan. Amazingly, the WWF went with almost exactly the same booking as the previous year, and Heenan scored the upset win with the help of nefarious heel tactics. The move didn't help elevate the Islanders, and team leader Haku soon split off on a solo career.

The Bulldogs got into a feud with hot tag champs Demolition as 1988 dragged on for them, but they were never in serious consideration to actually win and were merely used to give the champs the rub they were lacking. The Bulldogs continued their descent down the card—doing the opening match with the Rougeaus at the first Summerslam in 88, then closing out their WWF career by quietly losing in the tag team elimination match at Survivor Series 88. However, this rather innocuous exit has another story behind it.

Even more than their crazy moves in the ring, the Bulldogs were known for their crazier practical joking outside of it. Although Dynamite Kid was certainly the pioneer and the instigator in the early days, Davey Boy was a fast learner who soon became known as an equal terror to unsuspecting victims the world over. Putting laxatives in peoples' drinks was a favorite gag of theirs, but defiling bags in various (and increasingly disgusting) ways was another winner. While feuding with the Rougeaus late in 1988, Jacques became paranoid that they would become the target of a Bulldog prank (which was likely), so he asked Curt Hennig to guard his bag to make sure nothing happened to it. Hennig, himself a prankster, decided to double-cross Jacques by cutting his clothes to ribbons with a pair of scissors, then hiding out in the toilet to establish his alibi. What happened next varies according to the storyteller, but some details are consistent. Jacques immediately suspected the Bulldogs and confronted Dynamite. Dynamite, obsessed with maintaining his "hard man" image in front of the boys, slaps Jacques down and smashes his head into the floor twice, then beats on him until Raymond breaks it up. At this point, Dynamite knocks him out as well. Thinking that the matter is thus settled, Dynamite goes to shake hands with Jacques soon after the initial fight, but instead gets jumped with a sucker punch, aided by a foreign object of some sort (a roll of quarters according to some, brass knuckles according to Dynamite), which knocks out four teeth and by all rights should have put him down for the count. Amazingly, the Kid remains on his feet and willing to continue the fight until it's broken up.

Dynamite was strongly advised to let things be at that point, although he admits to a bit of petty revenge in his autobiography:

> I got a dentist's bill for $1800 and gave it to them. And the Rougeaus paid. But it wasn't my bill. I had my teeth fixed for nothing.

Vince himself warned against further retribution because Jacques was known for having a tough family, according to Dave Meltzer's book *Tributes II*. The Rougeaus were terrified of what Dynamite would do to them in the ring anyway, especially since the Bulldogs had now quit over the fight. Sympathetic Quebecois Pat Patterson booked the match so that the Rougeaus would lose five minutes into their Survivor Series elimination match, then booked the Bulldogs to go an additional thirty-five minutes, which gave the Rougeaus plenty of time to get to the airport and out of the area before the Bulldogs had a chance to go after them. And that ended the run of the British Bulldogs in the WWF.

Dynamite Kid was rapidly falling apart physically, and the relationship between the personable Smith and the injury-ridden Kid fell apart with it. The Bulldogs made one last try to salvage things by returning to their roots in Stampede Wrestling and its 500-person crowds in late 1988, which was a huge step down from the 20,000 seat arenas the WWF ran. To say this run was a disaster would be an understatement. The first problem was that Stampede was dying already and bringing in the Bulldogs was, at best, a desperation move with long odds of succeeding. The second problem was that Stu Hart, feeling the territory needed a change in direction, gave the book (creative control) to Dynamite Kid. Although they might have survived the first problem, it was the second one that really put the nail in the coffin on the territory.

Whereas Bruce Hart could be called many things as a booker—weird, over-the-top, slightly too far ahead of his time for his own good—Dynamite's approach to running things was a bit more direct and ham-fisted. Bloody brawls, chain matches, cage matches, street fights, whatever he could hotshot on a limited budget were the order of the day. He brought in aging WWF has-beens like Harley Race and Don Muraco and pushed them to the top because he knew them personally and respected them, regardless of fan perceptions of them as little more than midcard fodder. But the thing that really killed him was Ed Whalen.

Ed was more than the announcer for Stampede, he was its moral center. As news director and liaison to the CTV station that carried Stu's promotion, Ed literally held the fate of Stampede Wrestling in his hands, and testing him was usually a bad idea. Many years before, Bruce had pushed the envelope of violence with a street fight between Bad News Allen and Archie "Stomper" Gouldie, which resulted in blood spilling everywhere around the ring and fans nearly rioting. Two decades later most fans would barely bat an eyelash at the kind of low-level carnage that was on display there, but Whalen was an old-school fan to the extreme and disgustedly quit the promotion over the match. He took the show off the air as a result. Whalen would later return, but the point was made, and Bruce didn't push that far again. Dynamite, however, was more gung ho about things, and after the Bulldogs debuted and won the International tag team titles from Jerry Morrow & Cuban Assassin, his first major act was to split the team up and begin a feud with his cousin.

Now to say that no one wanted the Bulldogs to split up would be an understatement. I'm not just talking about the usual wussy fans who can't abide their heroes turning on each other, forget about them. This move annoyed far more important people, like Giant Baba of All-Japan, who was still paying the Bulldogs top dollar to draw money for his promotion while they were supposedly fighting each other in Stampede. The self-destruction of the team would have been likely anyway because they were having trouble getting along in real life due to Davey Boy's growing need to think for himself, which clashed with Dynamite's obsessive need to control every aspect of the team. From the number of times that he stresses in his book that "he was the leader of the team," I don't blame Smith one bit for wanting to get away from him. However, no matter how much Baba hated the breakup, Ed Whalen hated it more. Ed was the guy who championed their teaming in the first place back before either was a steroid-using freak, and Ed was probably the biggest fan left of the team. And when the Bulldogs as a team turned into Dynamite Kid & Johnny Smith v. Davey Boy Smith & Chris Benoit, Whalen quit Stampede and never returned.

Even that feud might have drawn some money (or least been one hell of a tag match), but for one last hiccup in the history of the promotion. Davey Boy Smith was in a van with Ross Hart, Chris Benoit, and Jason the Terrible when they hit a patch of ice and smashed into a station wagon. Davey went headfirst through the windshield (adding a lesson about seat belts on top of the ones about drugs) and ended any hope of coming back to wrestle in time to save the promotion. Things degenerated for Stampede rapidly after that, and wound up with ludicrous stories about Dynamite Kid attacking Bruce

Hart in a van on a spot show in the far north, overbounced pay-checks, and crappy working conditions. In the end, everyone left and the doors closed in December 1989.

For their part, the Bulldogs were still speaking enough to do one last tour of Japan, where Vince McMahon showed up for a cross-promotional effort. He asked the Bulldogs if they'd be interested in coming back to the U.S. again. Dynamite told him "when hell freezes over" and expected Davey to say the same, but instead he finally acted on his own and took Vince up on his offer. The Bulldogs never spoke again and Dynamite faded into retirement and obscurity a few months after, despite threats on his part of physical retaliation against Smith for "turning his back" on him.

The British Bulldogs because "The British Bulldog"—Davey Boy Smith.

Smith's new singles career didn't exactly rocket out of the gates; with the exception of their tours of Europe, he was used as a mid-card attraction for most of 1991. In England, he was a bona fide main event star and was given the fairly prestigious win in the Royal Albert Hall battle royale in October 1991. Even so, his career was flounder-ing outside of the English tour, and he was barely on the promotion radar for most of 1992. He wasn't even booked at Wrestlemania VIII, a show where everyone of note was shoehorned in somehow.

However, with WWE business doing great numbers in the U.K., Summerslam 92 was moved from its original location of Washington D.C. to Wembley Stadium. A previously announced match with Bret Hart defending the Intercontinental title against Shawn Michaels in a ladder match was changed to Bret defending the title against home-town boy Davey Boy Smith. This match resulted in a record-shattering attendance of 80,000 people filling the stadium and is the one time that Smith can truly claim that he drew a crowd almost single-handedly. Bret has since taken credit for at least half of that crowd, but Bret says a lot of things. That's what makes him Bret Hart. Davey, as well, thought that the match would be his defining moment, although Bret also claimed it as his own defining moment on his WWE-issued DVD. Either way it was a hell of a match.

How good the match actually was is a matter of some debate. I thought it was a fabulous match, one of my favorites of all time in fact, and I gave it the very rare ★★★★★ rating. Bret, however, feels differently, as he points out on his DVD that Davey Boy was blown up (out of breath) very early in the match and Bret had to literally do all the work for the majority of the match and essentially wrestling the match alone and leading Smith through the spots. He also produced slow-motion footage showing Davey missing vital spots. At that point, to me, it's just nit-picking. I really enjoyed the match as it was without feeling the need to go frame-by-frame like Bret felt the need to do, but you generally have to be a wrestler to get why the match was "flawed" in the first place. Regardless, Bret's story is that he went to Vince before the show and promised him the greatest Summerslam main event of all time if he booked it for Wembley, and that's what they delivered. Davey Boy pinned Bret after twenty-five minutes, reversing a sunset flip into a pinning combination to win the Intercontinental title. In retrospect, it was pretty much the peak of his career.

It does bring up another point with Davey, however, with regard to his conditioning for the match. Keeping in mind that his early career was spent flying all over the ring and keeping up with Dynamite Kid, it's striking how much heavier and bloated he had become by that point. Eager to obtain the same kind of ripped body that his cousin Dynamite had achieved, Davey had actually started on steroids as a teenager, which I think is a pretty clear indication of the kind of peer pressure, spoken or not, that existed in wrestling long before the WWF came along and turned it into The Look for all wrestlers. Davey had gone from flying around the ring with ease to being something of a clumsy power wrestler—overly muscled and slow.

As noted earlier, this new look for Davey quickly came around to bite him in the rear because federal investigators were leaning on Vince McMahon very heavily in the steroid trials of the '90s, and there were bound to be people thrown under the bus. So just two months after winning the title in the biggest show of his life, and one of the biggest shows in WWF history, Davey dropped the belt to Shawn Michaels on an episode of *Saturday Night's Main Event*. He went from conquering English hero to transitional champion just like that. But that's wrestling for you. Even worse for Davey, he got fingered for trafficking HGH to Ultimate Warrior, and was fired as a public gesture toward cleaning up the WWF's drug problems. However, because he was still a name value in the wrestling world, WCW was all too happy to sign him as soon as the ink on his release was dry and push him to the top, drugs or no.

In all fairness here, he was sold down the river by Vince McMahon without any real cause and wasn't partaking in anything that everyone else in the promotion didn't do themselves, so it's not like WCW was taking in a crack addict or anything. Smith's tenure there in 1993 probably won't be remembered for his in-ring performances (although there were some good ones) but rather for his involvement in some of the stupidest shit to ever be thought up by WCW. If you want hard evidence that drugs are widely in use in wrestling, WCW's booking could be submitted to a grand jury and get a conviction every time.

Example 1: Feeling that a tag team match between Sting, Davey Boy, Vader, and Sid Vicious was lacking a certain *je ne sais quois*, WCW's booking monkeys decided to spend $100,000 of Ted Turner's money to shoot a mini-movie so bad that people still bitch about it today. It featured Sid and Vader, the so-called Masters of the Powerbomb, terrorizing orphans on the beach (while wearing flip-flops like all supervillains do), until Sting and Smith swoop in to save the day and play volleyball with the kids. But wait! Cheatum the Evil Midget (that was honestly his name) tries to kill everyone with a bomb right out of a Tom & Jerry cartoon, which ended with a cliffhanger that left us unsure as to the fate of the babyfaces and the kids. As I've noted before, the true bomb was the *Bash at the Beach* PPV that was supposed to pay off this stupid angle, which barely drew enough money to cover the cost of the mini-movie.

Example 2: Sting and Smith team up again to face Vicious and Vader in the dreaded WarGames cage match at *Fall Brawl* in September 1993. However, they need a partner, so they recruit the former Tugboat/Typhoon, Fred Ottman. Booker Ole Anderson's idea is to recreate him as a mysterious superhero (an idea he was fixated on with Sting and the Black Scorpion in 1990 as well), so he's given a tinfoil-covered storm trooper helmet and dubbed The Shockmaster. His debut was to come on the live *Clash of the Champions* show that was building to the PPV, where he'd dramatically burst through the wall like the Kool-Aid Man and save the day for overpaid WWF rejects everywhere. Well, he burst through the wall all right and fell flat on his face on live TV, knocking his helmet off and leaving Davey Boy in tears of laughter for an angle that was supposed to be deadly serious and sell a show.

After months of getting lied to and screwed over, Smith no-showed some house shows and got fired shortly before he would have taken part in Starrcade 93, one of the few high points of that year for WCW. And so back to the WWF he went in 1994. Having left WCW as a main-eventer, Smith was now repushed upon his return and firmly established as a part of the upper echelon. He allied himself with Bret Hart in the war with brother-in-law Owen Hart, and was booked as the last guy to be eliminated in the 1995 Royal Rumble. He entered the match at number two and only lost out to Shawn Michaels, who had picked number one. Smith had actually lost a bit of muscle mass and was looking more human, but he bulked up again as a part of a team with Lex Luger dubbed the Allied Powers. Luger was representing America, Smith was representing the U.K., and their primary opponents were "Japanese" invader Yokozuna and Canadian Owen Hart, who perhaps should have "discovered" Nazi German roots to really drive the feud home. Either way, Smith bulked up again to keep up with Luger's body-in-a-bottle physique, and he also took on Luger's other characteristics: choking and bad luck. Although the team was obviously on the way to winning the tag titles, Lex Luger suddenly jumped back home to WCW in time for the first episode of Monday Nitro in 1995, leaving Smith without a partner and Vince looking stupid.

Perhaps to punish us for Luger's move, Davey Boy was suddenly pushed to the main event in a move that would have killed promotions with smaller cash reserves than the WWF had at the time. In Davey's first shot at the WWF World title on PPV, Smith and Kevin Nash absolutely stunk up the joint in the fourth *In Your House*, and the immediate result was Vince putting the title back on Bret for the time being. Davey got another shot, this time at Bret, and the result was another of the greatest matches in WWF history as they bled buckets of blood and didn't draw a dime.

But as Davey progressed up the card, he was also getting more involved in the seamier side of the business. He was notably involved in the infamous attack on Shawn Michaels in Syracuse, because Smith was a friend of the notorious Clique, Shawn's group of kiss-ass buddies who ran the WWF behind Vince McMahon's back. Davey was in a car when a group of marines called Shawn's big-mouthed bluff in a bar fight and beat the crap out of him, and Davey suffered some pretty good damage himself saving Shawn from what would have been a near-fatal beating had no one intervened.

Even worse for Davey, he faced legal trouble for another bar fight he was engaged in during 1993 in Calgary. A loud-mouthed patron named Kody Light claimed that Smith assaulted him and apparently threw him across the bar using a form of bodyslam or powerbomb, either of which would be very difficult to accomplish without the cooperation of the victim. Smith claimed that he choked Light from behind and let the bouncers deal with him. Either way, it was another black eye for wrestling as Smith was portrayed as a roid-raging maniac in the media, despite his eventual acquittal. His admission that everything in wrestling is fake was somehow a shocking story, even in 1996 when everyone pretty much knew it.

Oh, by the way, wrestling is fake, just in case you needed it clarified again.

Anyway, having failed to draw in main events against Bret Hart and Kevin Nash, they naturally decided to give Davey another kick at the can and this time against new champion Shawn Michaels. For you conspiracy types out there who think there really is a curse following Smith around since Stampede Wrestling, here's more evidence: Their big match at the *Beware of Dog* PPV, a show based around Bulldog's name, turned into the biggest debacle in WWF PPV history when the power went out halfway through the show and left viewers (myself included) staring at a black screen for half an hour while Vince McMahon freaked out and begged viewers not to switch channels because the main event was still coming. However, Shawn Michaels didn't used to be such a nice, well-adjusted Christian man and, not wanting to bother with the main event by that point, he also freaked out and threw a temper tantrum in the ring, The result was a jumbled mess of a match that was used to set up a rematch at *King of the Ring 96,* which was surrounded by a convoluted storyline about Smith's wife Diana Hart suing Michaels.

We'll get to Diana in a bit.

Things picked up for Davey again by the end of the year, as he and brother-in-law Owen Hart won the WWF World tag titles from the Smoking Gunns, Davey's first tag title with someone other than Dynamite Kid. This was actually quite a dominant reign, but being there weren't any serious contenders left for much of 1996 and 1997, it was probably more by default than anything. Think about it this way: One of their first major defenses was against the fake Razor Ramon and Diesel, and they seemed destined for a program with two guys from the AAA promotion in Mexico and/or feuding with each other until the WWF signed Doug Furnas and Phil LaFon to give them some good matches.

Speaking of having good matches, the WWF wanted to run tours of Europe again, and naturally wanted to promote Smith as their top guy over there. So the European championship was created and Smith won a tournament over partner Owen in Germany that was broadcast on a spectacularly low-rated edition of RAW. To be fair, it looked like something shot in the 1950s due to limitations of overseas broadcasting and bad lighting in the building, but it was one hell of a match. Over time it's become one of my all-time favorites, a total Japanese-style friend v. friend scientific battle with tons of cool reversals and a double-fakeout finish that acted as a callback to both of their classic encounters with Bret Hart. The title victory was seemingly building to a split of the tag champions and yet another lame feud between them but, instead, it built to something greater than the sum of its parts: The Hart Foundation.

We'll get to that whole thing in the Bret Hart section, but suffice it to say it was awesome and turned the company around. However, once again the peak of Davey's stay turned into another exit from the promotion for him. So he's the European champion and they want to run Europe with Davey on top, but things are bad between Vince and Bret. Real bad. And if you want political, check this out: They're running a show in England called *One Night Only*, solely for the consumption of British fans, with Bulldog defending his European title against Shawn Michaels, who was clearly back on the fast track to the World title. Negotiations for the finish in that match turned into a near fistfight as Bret insisted that Bulldog go over (what with his wife and dying sister at ringside and all), whereas Shawn and Vince wanted Shawn to go over so that Bulldog could win the title back at some nebulously defined point in the future that would never come. To say things were tense leading up to the match would be an understatement, and it's not even fair to choose sides because

everyone was being such jackasses to each other, like a divorce settlement. In the end, Vince is the boss and Shawn went over, and that
pretty much marked the end of the line for Davey.

Despite Smith's deteriorating body and increasing drug problems,
WCW still wanted to pay him upward of $100,000 a year for his for-
mer name. By this time, Smith, heavily dependent on a constant
stream of painkillers and with knees that were totally shot, was beyond a shell of his former self. The high point of his stay was a feud
with Steve McMichael, which produced the McMichael quote "Don't
just stand there drinking coffee when a man's talking to you!", and
not much else. After a few nondescript months in WCW, Smith took
a bad bump on a trapdoor built into the ring and suddenly blamed
years of injuries and drug use on WCW, as his already-crippled spine
put him in the hospital with an infection that nearly killed him. WCW,
with no real options left, fired him while he was still in the hospital, but somehow he managed to get yet another shot with the WWF
after Owen Hart died in 1999.

This time he was so broken down that he had to wear jeans to
the ring to disguise his massive leg braces, and he didn't venture
outside of the "Hardcore" style that basically limited him to kicking
and punching, except for a brief return to the main event against the
Rock that flopped spectacularly. Midway through 2000, divorced from
his wife and with his life falling apart, Smith was put into rehab by
the WWF, which then fired him for his accumulating drug problems.

I'd say that overall, Diana was pretty patient with him up until
then. A former beauty queen in her hometown of Calgary, Diana
worked for Stampede selling programs as a teenager and harbored
a secret crush on Dynamite Kid. When she couldn't attract his at-
tentions, she went after his cousin Davey Boy instead, and soon the
seventeen-year-old Diana, Stu's youngest daughter, and the eighteen-
year-old Davey Boy Smith were married. Although things seemed
fine from the outside for much of their marriage, the death of Owen

Hart in 1999 combined with Davey's years of drug abuse tore the entire family apart.

According to Diana, Davey, who needed money after the car accident that had nearly killed him, had gotten mixed up with a drug dealer named Hermesh Erach Austin as early as 1990. Ben Bassarab, another Hart-in-law, had been so wrapped up with Austin that he ended up serving eighteen months in prison with him on a drug bust before disassociating himself from him. Apparently fearing for his life, Davey continued his attempts to stay on Austin's good side even after the prison term. And with good reason it seems, as Austin ended up in prison again for kidnapping, torturing, and murdering a man who had supposedly stolen money from him. Diana doesn't know how far Davey got into debt with Austin, but it's probably quite lucky for him that Austin ended up meeting the fate he did.

Even worse was Davey's spiraling addictions, which were destroying their marriage in stages. The years of steroids and growth hormone were the most obvious culprits, with Davey carrying 270 pounds of muscle on a body made for 200. But after the back injury in WCW in 1998, Davey also picked up a growing addiction to morphine. Diana relates stories about Smith being so stoned that he was only able to sit at the table and drool, while she was forced to squirt him with a water pistol to bring him back to attention enough to feed himself. Her solution was an overdose of Xanax (one of the meds found in Johnny Grunge's system after his death), which finally shocked Davey into checking into rehab.

Sadly, the story had no happy ending. If anything, it got more pathetic, as Diana divorced him in 2000 even while son Harry was himself training to become a wrestler. Davey was very supportive and trained him for his debut; but while playing loving father on one side, he was also engaged in the low point of the Hart family. Their white trash antics peaked when Bruce Hart's wife Andrea left Bruce in favor of Davey Boy, which pretty much tore the family apart for good. Davey finished rehab, but was in total denial about his drug problem up until the day he died, May 17, 2002. On a positive note, he had just teamed with Harry Smith in a tag team match to debut his son to the wrestling world, hopefully not another victim of the same curse that plagued him and his partner their whole careers.

The official cause of death for Davey was the usual heart attack caused by a lifetime of steroid use, but really he had been destroying his life, match by match, ever since the first day that his cousin shot him up with steroids. The Bulldogs were a doomed team, in my opinion, as Dynamite himself disappeared off the face of the earth shortly after Davey Boy's death, having never again spoken to his cousin and former closest friend in the business.

I think saddest and most telling of all is the concluding statement of Dynamite's autobiography. It's worth reprinting to put their careers in perspective, I think.

I'd do it all again. I wouldn't change a thing. Wrestling was my life, and I loved it. No regrets. I had a blast.

Well, there's your problem.

BRIAN PILLMAN

Perhaps one of the worst stories to come from Stampede's doomed crop of great wrestlers was that of "Flyin" Brian Pillman. Some wrestlers died young and in their prime before they could fall apart. Some wrestlers died when their careers were over, and they weren't expected to stay in wrestling shape anyway. Pillman was more tragic than either of those scenarios. He was a guy who started out so young and vital, and you could see the combination of the wrestling business and the drugs eating away at him like a cancer as he got older. He was transformed from a bright young star in 1989 to an embittered and broken down addict by 1996, who desperately clung to the only business he knew and fell apart before our very eyes. I'd like to say people were shocked and horrified when he was found dead in a hotel room on October 6, 1997, but really the only question left was whether he was trying one last con job on us by faking his own death as an ultimate work. Sadly, he wasn't.

Pillman was born May 22, 1962 in Ohio, which would remain his billed home for his whole career. Right away you could tell that this poor kid was in for a rough go of it, because he was born with a form of throat cancer and as a baby had to endure thirty-one different operations on his vocal cords to remove it. This condition would leave him with the raspy voice that became one of his trademarks later in his career and set the stage for his underdog career. Although he was better known for his football prowess in his school life, his initial passion was for hockey but his small hometown of Norwood didn't have a hockey program. Instead, he concentrated on football and joined the Miami of Ohio team as a walk-on and surprised everyone by becoming an All-American thanks to his stubborn attitude and steroids. His steroid use got him up to 230 pounds, but it wasn't enough to get him into the NFL draft. So again he had to fight for a spot by trying out with the Cincinnati Bengals and surviving the endless rounds of punishment that they put tryouts through. He made the team for the 1984 season and gained something of a reputation as a crazy "wedge-buster," who sacrificed himself to break through the defense. Still, in the grand scheme of things, he was just too small to be in the NFL, and the Bengals traded him to the Buffalo Bills before the 1985 season. Although he might have continued to disguise his size with the roids, the Bills didn't want to take a chance with him and cut him loose. He wound up in the Canadian Football League, making a name for himself in Calgary by playing with the Stampeders, but a broken ankle ended his football career quickly into his CFL run.

Pillman's mentor, and the Bengals' strength coach, Kim Wood, gave him the name of the Hart Family, and once again Stu Hart's love of football players became a factor. Pillman applied his same maniacal training methods to wrestling that he did to football, and he studied tapes like a madman while training for his new career as a pro wrestler. Initially he came in as a Calgary Stampeder, with the team being special guests of the Hart Family, and they did a typical wrestling angle whereby main heels Makhan Singh and Great Gama would attack him and set up a tag team match between themselves and the team of Pillman and two of the Hart brothers. Pillman, who was a fast learner in and out of the ring, was an instant star in Stampede Wrestling and he became a regular attraction for the promotion. In one of those odd bits of serendipity that wrestling produces, an early storyline saw them hiring an actress named Teresa Hayes to play his "sister" for a one-shot angle where the heels attacked her before she disappeared again. However, she only disappeared for six years. After trying her hand at modeling and acting for a few years, she returned to wrestling by sheer chance as Beulah McGillicuddy in ECW and eventually married WWE wrestler Tom "Tommy Dreamer" Laughlin.

Anyway, Pillman's run in Stampede was one that had a huge influence on me as his development as a wrestler somewhat followed that of two of my other heroes as a teen, Chris Benoit and Owen Hart. The three of them were young kids growing up in Stampede, and as a young fan it was always tremendously fascinating for me to watch such obvious future stars at the beginning of their career, because it gave me a feeling of ownership and homegrown pride that was difficult if not impossible to find with the larger and more impersonal WWF. Pillman teamed up with Stampede booker Bruce Hart as Bad Company, and they quickly dominated the International tag team titles, although it wasn't until much later that I would come to realize why exactly they were so rarely beaten and why Bruce Hart tended to get the winning pin most of the time. I was young, what can I say? Although Owen Hart was the resident high-flyer of Stampede, Pillman developed his own high-risk style and became a star in his own right, although always in the shadow of Bruce Hart and never really as a single.

By 1989, Pillman got the number of WCW booker Jim Ross and asked about coming there, and they actually had big plans for him. He was originally planned as a replacement for Randy Rose in the original Midnight Express team with Dennis Condrey. But as usual the only constant at WCW was idiotic changes, and a booking team change resulted in that idea getting scrapped and Pillman coming in as a generic pretty boy babyface instead. Pillman, who at least by then had the knack of making exactly the right friends in the business, got in tight with Ric Flair and was portrayed on TV as Flair's protégé for a while, and they even went so far as to claim that Flair had trained him to be a wrestler. Still, in the end, Pillman was small and wrestlers are generally big, and even roiding up to 250 pounds and wrestling an exciting style wasn't enough to overcome that. Not that he didn't try, as a run with Tom Zenk as a generic pretty boy team in 1990 got them the U.S. tag team titles and a feud with the Midnight Express that produced some choice matches. He was also fairly successful as a singles wrestler early on, riding the momentum of his rub from Flair into a U.S. title match against Lex Luger at *Halloween Havoc 89* and managing to get a ★★★★ match out of Luger. Ironically, everyone in WCW was hoping that Luger would carry Pillman to a good match, when anyone with half a brain (i.e., anyone not running WCW at the time) knew it would be the exact opposite. Although that match and his tag title run seemingly established him as a heavyweight threat, he was continually shoehorned into the light-heavyweight division.

Although Pillman was small, he was well known for being tough, which Sid Vicious discovered in 1991. WCW had a big show in the Meadowlands arena in January that featured an undercard match where Sid essentially squashed the smaller Pillman like a jobber, because that's the way it was at that point. It was nothing personal on Sid's part, although Pillman took it quite personally because he had come up in the business by facing down bigger and dumber football players than Sid, and he had developed a mindset against people telling him what he couldn't do because of his size. The situation between them worsened at the *WrestleWar 91* PPV, as they faced each other on the opposite sides of teams involved in a WarGames match. The gimmick involved a roof on the top of a cage, and the finish ended up being botched by Sid, as he powerbombed Pillman and misjudged the height of the ceiling. Pillman's head hit the roof of the cage and then Sid dropped him straight on his head on the mat, nearly breaking his neck in the process. And then he picked Pillman up and delivered another powerbomb, not realizing the severity of what he had just done. The agents improvised a new finish on the spot, fearing for Pillman's life, and the heel team was awarded the win because Pillman was unable to continue. Things might have contin-

ued to worsen between Pillman and Sid, had Sid not made an inevitable jump to the WWF two months later. That move would have
normally killed the bad blood, but one night in October 1991 the two
promotions were running the same city, and Sid was drunk and bragging to a bar full of wrestlers about all the money he was making
and the main events he was wrestling. Pillman, representing WCW and
the little guy, took exception to Sid's big talk and decided to take
him down like he was a college quarterback who was making fun
of him. Sid, immediately overwhelmed by the psychotic Pillman,
showed his true colors and ran away from the fight, only to return
with the only weapon he could find in the parking lot: a squeegee.
Luckily, agents on hand quickly intervened and took the deadly
weapon away before anyone's window could be inadvertently cleaned,
but the confrontation turned Pillman into an instant locker-room legend.

Pillman's fight with Sid might have convinced the boys that he
was worthy to hang with the heavyweights, but the bookers still considered him a lightweight and booked him as such. But hey, that was
good for us fans, as he got to wrestle fellow Stampede alumnus Jushin
"Thunder" Liger every night at the end of 1991. Liger, who started
in Calgary under his real name, Keichi Yamada, is one of the few
survivors of that class of the late 1980s who not only avoided the
pitfalls of the business but is still a huge star today in Japan. Still, the
curse is not so easily avoided as Liger was diagnosed with a brain
tumor in 1996, the removal of which left him with hearing in only
one ear. Small price to pay compared to others from the promotion,
I suppose.

Pillman won the first ever WCW Lightheavyweight title at *Halloween Havoc 91* by defeating Ricky Morton in the finals of a lame
tournament. This boring match was notable only for the referee wearing a camera on his head in one of the stranger ideas WCW ever
had. Although well-paid, Pillman's career as a plucky babyface was
going nowhere, and after dropping the belt to newcomer Scotty

Flamingo (Scott Levy, the future Raven), he started the heel turn that would redefine his career. However, when WCW again changed bookers and Bill Watts came in, Pillman's inflated contract became a point of contention, as Watts was not noted for pushing smaller wrestlers. Watts demanded that Pillman renegotiate or be relegated to jobbing for the rest of his contract, and Pillman famously retorted that he'd just have to be the highest-paid curtain-jerker in wrestling history. Although Pillman was a hot act and a big attraction for WCW, he lost every night in the opening match until it became obvious that neither side was going to back down. Watts was stubborn but not stupid, and once it became too much of an embarrassment to continue the petty punishment, Pillman's heel turn was put into high gear and he was repackaged as a tag team wrestler with Steve Austin for lack of anything better to do with the two of them. Although both were initially hesitant about the idea, they later became good partners and eventually best friends, and the team nearly revitalized tag team wrestling for a while. But originally Austin was put with Barry Windham, which made for a very different dynamic, more of a tough Texan team.

At *Starrcade 92*, Austin and Windham made their debut by challenging new champions Ricky Steamboat and Shane Douglas for the titles, and lost in a hard-fought match. Windham, however, was promised a push to the NWA World title at that point, which left Austin without a partner. Austin was given Brian Pillman as a partner and essentially told to do whatever they wanted to create their own characters, because WCW had bigger and better things to worry about. Pillman and Austin proceeded to create just that by playing a pair of arrogant jerks who so blatantly lied, cheated, and stole every victory (complete with "movie camera" motions to mock the opponents and fake knee injuries at every chance) that they suddenly became the biggest thing going in WCW. They even had a catch phrase: "Your brush with greatness is over."

They were dubbed the Hollywood Blonds, and now Pillman's

personality finally started to shine through. Whereas he had been playing the blond-haired babyface for the past three years, it was the arrogant scumbag heel that was closer to his true calling. In fact, Pillman's womanizing and partying exploits were the stuff of legend in a business where getting drunk every night and doing a bottle of pills while screwing three ringrats at a time is considered a warmup. The joke most associated with Pillman is that although you used to read the letters in the Penthouse Forum and wondered if they were real or fake, the truth is that they were all real and all written by Pillman. It was that lowlife spirit that shone through in the Blonds team, as Austin and Pillman just gave off the arrogant aura of two guys who knew they were better than everyone else in the promotion and weren't afraid to say it. And they probably were, because the matches they had with WCW tag team champions Shane Douglas and Ricky Steamboat were also the stuff of legends, nearly hitting the coveted ★★★★★ mark on a regular basis until WCW finally pulled the trigger and put the belts on the Blonds in March of 1993 after two months of booking them to chase the champions. It looked like they were going to be the greatest team of the '90s, the team that would replace the Midnight Express as the standard for heel teams everywhere, but it wasn't to be.

Austin and Pillman's defining moment as heels came when they mocked Ric Flair's interview segment and renamed it "A Flair for the Old" and used a statue to portray Arn Anderson. Instantly the Blonds were the biggest heels in the promotion, but it was to be short-lived because WCW didn't want them getting over. Although they built a hot feud between the Blonds and the returning Ric Flair, politics and paranoia interjected, and to this day each of the "old-timers" who ran the company blames the other old-timers for being the ones to sabotage their push. The excuse was that the much-hyped blowoff between the Horsemen and the Blonds on TBS drew only a 2.6, the lowest rating for a Clash of Champions special ever, and someone had to take the blame because god knows the bookers were all perfect human beings. The Blonds were put into a program with Arn Anderson and Paul Roma for the tag titles, and it was there that WCW did their first internet swerve. You may recall the Disney tapings of 1993, when WCW gave away all the title switches for the three-month period in one taping. Well, one of those changes had Anderson and Roma winning the tag titles from the Blonds. And they just happened to have a match coming up at *Beach Blast 93*, so everyone assumed that it would be the title change. In fact it was supposed to be but, just to swerve the Internet fans, WCW changed it to the Blonds going over instead. They were only able to pat themselves on the back for cleverness long enough to find out that Brian Pillman was now injured and they had two weeks to change the titles before shows with the Horsemen as champions started airing. Oops. The elegant solution: Substitute Steven Regal for Pillman on a Clash of the Champions show and job the makeshift team to Anderson & Roma. And that was that for the Hollywood Blonds, as Austin was informed that he would be getting a singles push and Pillman would be turning face.

Pillman's disaster of a personal life started catching up with him by 1993 while his career fell apart, as he was involved with a girlfriend named Rochelle who was one of those chicks that your mother warned you about. Specifically, the type who has your kid and then embroils you in a custody battle straight out of the Jerry Springer show. Pillman was no angel and his drug exploits were talked about in the locker room many times, but he was a rank amateur next to Rochelle, who was often seen hanging around the seedier side of Cincinnati shopping for drugs. The custody battle got vicious, with accusations on both sides (Pillman accused her of being an incurable addict, Rochelle accused him of sexually abusing their daughter), and in the middle of the fight Rochelle suddenly disappeared. Pillman was the lead suspect in the police's mind and ended up getting brought in on a minor drunk driving charge while under suspicion, which probably didn't help his case. Rochelle eventually surfaced in

Florida, a complete mess, and lost the custody battle to Pillman as a result. Pillman eventually married a former Penthouse Pet named Melanie, but even she got dragged into his horrific personal life when Rochelle called her one night in 1996, wanting to talk to Brian and threatening to commit suicide. Unfortunately, Brian was wrestling that night and wasn't around. Although Melanie did her best to talk Rochelle out of it, Rochelle called her mother right after their conversation and shot herself in the head, taking her own life as the ultimate revenge against Pillman.

Brian was seemingly becoming less stable himself, and a severe back injury suffered in 1994 left him essentially on the sidelines of the promotion for most of the year, jobbing in opening matches on PPV and drifting aimlessly as a bland babyface. His most notable match, again in the opening slot, came on the very first edition of WCW's new Monday Nitro in September 1995 as he wrestled old foe Jushin Liger in a short but good match that ultimately meant nothing. Much like with the Blonds, Pillman was clearly going to have to take matters into his own hands if he wanted to recreate his career. Luckily for him, he was still friends with Ric Flair and WCW was still obsessed with trying to reinvent the Four Horsemen until every last cent had been milked out of that concept. Pillman, who had gotten all the mileage out of the Flyin Brian concept that he was going to get, went back to the spirit of the Hollywood Blonds and began to formulate his own gimmick and hopefully get himself over, since management was unwilling to put any further effort into him with the end of his contract rapidly approaching. His solution was a historic one, as he transformed himself into "The Loose Cannon," letting only Eric Bischoff and a select few members of the booking committee know about his plans. The idea, still a new one at that point and not the hackneyed cliché that it became in later years, would be to "work the boys" and have Pillman act as unpredictably as possible, so that no one, fans or wrestlers alike, would have any idea what Pillman would do next. His plans ranged from a staged backstage fight with Bischoff to attending a Bengals game and hand-cuffing himself to the goalposts to draw attention to himself. Because he wasn't the biggest guy in the business, he at least wanted to be known as the craziest. Although neither of those ideas panned out, his reputation for manic behavior on live TV was made forever dur-ing a match with Eddie Guerrero on a *Clash of the Champions* special when he ran to ringside and harassed commentator Bobby Heenan at a random point in the match. Heenan, who had often made it known that his neck surgery left him an absolute hands-off nonpar-ticipant in the proceedings at ringside, freaked out at possibly being assaulted by the crazed Pillman and uttered a shocked "What the fuck are you doing?" on live TV, visibly shaken up by the "attack."

As part of his character makeover, the increasingly heelish Pill-man began hanging out with Arn Anderson, who was in the midst of a breakup angle with long-time companion Ric Flair. Sure, you could see this one coming from a mile away, but many of the newer fans of the promotion likely hadn't been around the last time they did that storyline in 1990. So as it went, Flair recruited Sting to help him in the war against Arn and Brian, and promised not to turn on him all the way, but then turned on him to re-form the Four Horse-men. There's a whole conversation to have on how dumb the Sting character was to keep falling for it, but we don't really have the time. With the addition of Chris Benoit, the Horsemen were complete, but now booker Kevin Sullivan wanted to be a part of the strangely in-triguing Loose Cannon gimmick. In reality, Pillman's gimmick was one that was never going to be allowed to draw a dime, but WCW as an entity was seemingly obsessed with fooling fans and employ-ees alike in the name of unpredictability. The on-screen climax of the storyline happened at *SuperBrawl VI*, when Pillman was supposed to be wrestling Kevin Sullivan in a "respect" match, in which the loser had to say they respected the winner to end the match. Pillman, barely a minute into the match, grabbed the microphone and gave his famous quote: "I respect you, bookerman!" This exclamation would have been a major no-no had everyone in the office not already been in on the joke, because you didn't say words like "booker" on live TV in 1996 and escape with your job intact. Bischoff and Sullivan figured that was the end of it, and Pillman would be "fired" and take some time in ECW to hone the character before coming back. And because no one else but those two knew about the true nature of the storyline, it seemed to be a perfect plan.

And then Pillman decided to push things one step further.

His reasoning was that if working a few people got him a little buzz, then double-crossing the boss would get him big money when he returned to WCW after trashing them for a few weeks in ECW. So he talked Bischoff into firing him for real, to really drive home the angle. But there's "real" and then there's really real. Bischoff thought he was giving Pillman some real-looking paperwork and sending him off to ECW on a secret deal. But because no one else in the office knew about that secret deal, he had outsmarted himself and given Pillman his actual release which freed him up to negotiate with anyone. He played the WWF and WCW off each other, until he had an offer upward of $400,000 a year on the table from both sides thanks to a hot run in ECW. However, once he signed with the WWF and he was on the verge of the biggest push of his career as the next opponent for WWF champion Shawn Michaels, his life fell apart again. After a night of binge drinking and drugs, he crashed his Humvee and destroyed his face and ankle, which probably should have ended his career. However, to his advantage, business was in the toilet for the WWF and they needed a ratings boost badly enough that they still offered a guaranteed contract (the first one in WWF history) and waited out his recovery. It proved to be a disaster, as a feud with Steve Austin quickly fizzled thanks to rushing back into the ring, and he had to have another surgery on his ankle to repair the damage he had done coming back from the first one. This incident at least gave him a place in history, as he was written out of the storylines via an attack by Steve Austin with a chair that "broke his ankle." This came to be known as "Pillmanizing" someone, although to date Webster's dictionary has yet to add it.

Whereas WCW's approach with Pillman's crazed character was to play mind games with their own employees, the WWF chose to mess with the fans instead, because that's how they roll. In this case, a recovering Pillman continued his feud with Austin in a staged confrontation on RAW when Austin stalked Pillman to his home in order to build up both men as badasses who wouldn't back down. In Pillman's case, he chose to defend his home by pulling a gun on the invading Austin, and the show ended with an ominous gunshot that left viewers with the assumption that someone had been shot dead. For some reason, the USA Network had a problem with that cliffhanger and the WWF was made to apologize immediately, something that certainly has never come easy for Vince McMahon. Just ask Bret Hart. Pillman was taken off TV for a while to take the heat off him, but once he was fairly recovered he was brought back for the hottest angle of 1997—the Hart Foundation.

Although this was probably the peak of Pillman's career, he was done as a wrestler. His second ankle surgery had fused his shattered ankle into a walking position, leaving him barely able to run the ropes, let alone wrestle a proper match. He was in intense pain everyday, and was falling apart right before our eyes—looking like a strung out junkie during his promos and experimenting with stronger and stronger painkillers. Things were getting really bad between him and Melanie, as he constantly resisted going to rehab, triggered fights, and made the situation worse. His attitude was summed up best by a shirt that he would wear to annoy his wife that said "Rehab is for quitters." Showing all the signs of paranoia and self-loathing that addicts often demonstrate, Pillman was also falling apart professionally. All attempts to get him into rehab were perceived by Pillman as a betrayal by his friends, and all the people who had previously been his actual friends were afraid to be around him any longer.

In the end Pillman was involved in a sleazy midcard angle with

Goldust, where he would win Terri Runnels as his love slave and eventually steal her away from her real-life husband in favor of a kinky sex relationship with Pillman. This was all too close to home for Dustin "Goldust" Runnels, who was not only well aware of Pillman's reputation for kinky sex but of Pillman's former real-life relationship with Terri. Lucky for him, I guess, that Brian Pillman was found dead on October 5, with a pharmacy of prescription pills lying around the room.

Pillman's death at least had some positive impact in the long run, as pill doctor Joel Hackett was banned from WWF locker rooms as a result of his prescribing the meds to Brian. Melanie was given a generous amount of help from the WWF and also got a cut of the proceeds from the annual Brian Pillman Memorial shows staged by Les Thatcher. However, she eventually remarried and lost the sympathies of the wrestlers who were supposed to be assisting her in her time of need. In the end, the person helped most by the shows was William Regal, who managed to get his career back on track after a history of drug use and won a job with the WWF again thanks to an epic match with Chris Benoit. I guess that's something.

Clearly Pillman was a guy who felt pressured by the business to start on a drug plan and continue using them to keep up with the Joneses. He had a long-time complex about being the smaller guy, and he used HGH and steroids to compensate for that. Melanie has said that she believes HGH played a part in his heart attack, although an autopsy showed it to be congenital and merely accelerated by the drugs. Pillman was another in an endless line of guys who used up his last chance and should have retired while he was able, and the heartless business killed him for giving everything to it.

Although it might be easier to remember the more shocking moments, like Vince McMahon announcing before the *Badd Blood* PPV that Pillman was dead but the show had to go on, I'd like to remember my favorite Pillman moment instead. It was the *Canadian Stampede* show in July, and the main event was the five-man team of the Hart Foundation against Steve Austin's team, and the Harts were heroes in Calgary. Pillman, who had been feeding off the hatred of fans for years with his crazy heel character, was the first one introduced, and he was suddenly greeted to a thunderous ovation unlike anything he'd ever experienced before. It was the look of someone who was finally happy after years of despair and breaking down mentally and physically, and I think Pillman would have stood there soaking it in all night had they let him. That's how I prefer to remember him.

BRET HART

Bret Hart was faced with a different type of curse and yet the same one deep down. In one sense he was the most successful of his family, winning five WWF World championships and two in WCW, but he ended up as the victim of his own success.

Born into the huge Hart family in July 1957, Bret was never interested in pursuing the pro-wrestling lifestyle, despite the overwhelming influence of his brothers and father. He was a champion wrestler in high school and did some occasional refereeing for his father's Stampede Wrestling, but his career goal was to be a director, to which end he entered the Mount Royal College of Film. However, when that didn't work out, he had a spot waiting for him in wrestling and proved to be a natural. Despite his untraditional look and physique, he proved to be the most popular and talented of all the Harts. He won the North American title six times from 1980–1983 and had some shockingly violent matches with Bad News Allen, including the first ever ladder match in wrestling.

When the WWF bought out Stampede in the early '80s, Bret made the jump to them, along with brother-in-law and family friend Jim Neidhart. Lacking in personality and style, Bret began as a jobber wearing very unfashionable black tights. Seeing Bret's potential, the WWF teamed him with Neidhart and made Memphis import Jimmy Hart their manager to talk for them. They were dubbed The Hart Foundation. The focus on the team in the early days was the psychotic Jim Neidhart's act, and Bret provided the solid wrestling foundation to carry the team in the background. They were entered in the wrestler-football player battle royale at Wrestlemania 2 and ended up as the last two men eliminated, both by Andre the Giant. Bret's technical skills were starting to turn some important heads by this point, and he was given the nickname "Excellence of Execution" by announcer and WWF honcho Gorilla Monsoon. A push was soon to follow as Bret rapidly adjusted to the more fast-paced and entertainment-based style of the WWF. The tights changed to the more familiar pink-and-black colors, and he added his trademark wraparound shades for that true "Hitman" look.

The Harts spent much of 1986 challenging the British Bulldogs for the tag titles, but were never considered a serious threat. They also had a mini-feud going with the Killer Bees over the number one contender spot, which was generally won by the Bees. Oddly enough, the Harts got most of the title shots out of the deal. With the total deterioration of Dynamite Kid as 1986 drew to a close, the WWF wanted to go with a heel tag team champion to replace them for a long run, and the Hart Foundation were given that chance. With the help of crooked referee Danny Davis, the Harts stole the tag titles from the Bulldogs and became the number one team in the promotion. Davis joined them as an unofficial member and general lackey, and teamed up with them for a six-man match at Wrestlemania III against the Bulldogs and Tito Santana. Davis got the fluke pin on Davey Boy Smith to win the match, and the Harts ended up with huge heel heat out of the match.

During this period, Bret Hart's rep as a singles wrestler was given a sudden boost as well. The Harts had been doing some flunkying for the Honky Tonk Man, which included beating up Randy Savage in the attack that led to the formation of the Megapowers. This attack, however, led to a match between Savage and Bret on SNME, easily the best one of Bret's WWF career and on a high-profile show no less. This match began building something of an "underground" following for Bret, who had always been regarded as the weak link in the team before that point. Now, Bret was clearly becoming the focus of the team and Neidhart was simply the hired muscle.

Bret Hart's face turn was continued at the first-ever Royal Rumble in January 1988, as he set the first longevity record at twenty-five minutes after drawing number 2. The official turn came at Wrestlemania IV, as he was entered in the battle royale that kicked off the show. It came down to Bret, Bad News Brown (aka his old nemesis Bad News Allen from Stampede), and the Junkyard Dog. Bret and Brown formed a heel alliance to eliminate JYD but, since there's no honor among heels, Brown turned on Hart and won the thing himself. This outcome had the effect of both turning Bret face and getting him away from Jim Neidhart long enough to start a singles push for him. Bret and Brown's only major match occurred at the special "WrestleFest" card in Milwaukee in 1988, where Brown outsmarted Hart and got the win. But the seeds were planted in the WWF's mind for a Bret singles push, and he kept getting the occasional singles match to hone his skills in that area.

Meanwhile, the Hart Foundation was turned into a tag team again, and this time they fired Jimmy Hart as their manager. Hart retaliated by siding with the Fabulous Rougeau Brothers and then upped the ante by selling one half of the Hart Foundation's WWF contract to the Rougeaus, which essentially gave the heels control of the Harts' bookings, in storyline terms, for a few weeks. Jimmy Hart caused the Harts to lose their tag title match at Summerslam 88, and the whole situation built to Hart Foundation & "Hacksaw" Jim Duggan v. The Rougeaus & Dino Bravo at the Royal Rumble 89. The Harts won that one in two straight falls and then beat Honky Tonk Man & Greg Valentine at Wrestlemania V. The Hart Foundation spent most of 1989 in total career limbo, losing as many as they won and not doing anything of note aside from being "senior team on the totem pole" to act as a measuring stick for new contenders to the titles. Bret Hart did several singles matches for WWF's home videos during this period to fill the time, which included an excellent draw with Ted Dibiase. The Harts lost a non-title match at Summerslam 89 to new champions Tully Blanchard & Arn Anderson, but were then split up in time for Survivor Series. Bret Hart was put on Jim Duggan's team and jobbed to Randy Savage in short order, but the pop his entrance got was not ignored.

The Hart Foundation squashed the Bolsheviks in eight seconds at Wrestlemania VI and made it known that they wanted a shot at Demolition for the tag titles. In response, Demolition added a third member to their ranks: Crush. In reality, Ax (Bill Eadie) was aging and suffering from a heart problem and the WWF didn't have the confidence (or medical insurance) to send him on the road every night and risk a heart attack mid-ring. The Smash and Crush duo were actually superior to the original Ax and Smash in some ways, but Crush's lack of experience and credibility with the fans weighed them down in the end. The title match came at Summerslam 90, and The Hart Foundation won the tag titles in two straight falls. Following Summerslam, the WWF was in financial disarray and began handing out the pink slips. Wisely deciding that Jim Neidhart was no longer worth the money being paid, he was fired in October and the Harts lost the tag titles to the Rockers in the infamous "phantom title reign" match. The belts were returned when the WWF changed their minds and Bret's singles push was delayed yet again. Bret drew number one in the 1991 Royal Rumble to showcase him on his own for the fans, and he impressed a great many of them. In fact, Bret was now more over in his minimal singles appearances than much of the midcard was in their regular ones, so as 1991 began the WWF finally pulled the trigger on the Bret Hart singles push. The Hart Foundation lost the tag titles to the Nasty Boys at Wrestlemania VII, and Neidhart was fired soon after. Bret Hart did a double-countout with Ted Dibiase on Saturday Night's Main Event in April as a dry run, and he was still very over with the fans. So they went to the next stage with him.

At Summerslam 91, Bret defeated Mr. Perfect to win his first major singles title, winning the Intercontinental title by blocking a legdrop and hooking his new finisher: The Sharpshooter. Bret had been taught the move by Mexican star Konnan during the time when Konnan was portraying "Max Moon" in the WWF, and the move quickly became the premiere submission move in the WWF. Bret's reign was an instant sensation, and he quickly became one of the most popular stars in the WWF without Neidhart to anchor him down. In fact, by January 1992, WCW was making overtures for his services when his contract expired. Just in case Bret "tried" something on PPV like Honky Tonk Man attempted on live TV almost four years earlier to the day, the title was taken off Bret and put on The Mountie (Jacques Rougeau) at a house show two days prior to the Royal Rumble (where Bret was to defend against the Mountie again). Because Mountie was little more than a comedy jobber at that point, the WWF claimed that Bret had the flu and thus his game was off that night. Roddy Piper got the shot at the Mountie at the PPV and won the title easily. After signing Bret to a new long-term deal, just in case, this set up a face vs. face confrontation between Piper and Bret at Wrestlemania VIII, and Bret regained the title from Piper in a very good match. It also had the effect of using Piper's stardom to elevate Hart yet again. And elevate him they soon would, because Bret was becoming a phenomenon in his own right: A wrestler who got over not on gimmicks or interviews or soap opera but on wrestling. He went out and gave it his all and the fans loved him. Bret was a throwback to a prior era thanks to the work ethic instilled by his father, Stu Hart, and it paid off as Bret kept climbing the ranks. Ultimately, that same philosophy would destroy his life. Bret did another face v. face match, and this time against brother-in-law Davey Boy Smith at Summerslam 92 in Smith's home country of England. In front of 80,000 people at Wembley Stadium, Smith blocked a sunset flip and pinned Hart to win the I-C title. But bigger things were in store for Bret.

After puttering around the midcard for a few months, Bret was suddenly informed out of nowhere while doing a TV taping in Saskatchewan that the entire direction of the WWF was changing, and that aging stars like Hulk Hogan and Ric Flair were going to be phased out and Bret was going to be phased in. He was put over WWF champion Ric Flair that very night, and was now the WWF champion to the shock of millions. Hart immediately began defending against every contender who wanted a shot, night after night, quickly earning a rep as the most hard-working champion the WWF had seen in some time. He beat Razor Ramon at Royal Rumble 93 and would have gone over Yokozuna at Wrestlemania IX had the Hulk Hogan situation not interjected itself, which left Bret to job the title in a shortened match and hope for a rematch down the road with Hogan. One never came. By way of consolation, Bret was given the King of the Ring tournament win in June 1993, beating Razor Ramon, Mr. Perfect, and finally Bam Bam Bigelow to take the crown. However, following that win, announcer Jerry "The King" Lawler, taking exception to someone other than him being "King," attacked Hart and stole his crown. Lawler verbally tormented Bret on Monday Night RAW for weeks following, taking cheapshot after cheapshot at him until finally a match was set for Summerslam 93 between the two. Lawler initially attempted to duck out of the match by claiming a "broken leg" and sending Doink the Clown to take his place. After Bret dispatched Doink, Lawler himself was forced into the match by WWF President Jack Tunney and was beaten senseless by Hart to the delight of the fans. However, Bret refused to release the Sharpshooter and got disqualified, making Lawler the undisputed King. A gigantic pull-apart brawl with the entire Hart family storming the ring resulted, and a rematch was on the horizon.

It was supposed to be at Survivor Series 93, with Bret and brothers Keith, Bruce, and Owen taking on Lawler and his three masked "Knights" (Barry Horowitz, Greg Valentine, and Jeff Gaylord), but complications arose. Mere weeks before that show, a 13-year-old Memphis girl accused Lawler of raping her, and Lawler was indicted on the charge. His name was cleared but not soon enough to make the show, and Shawn Michaels took his place. The match, which featured the Harts systematically taking out all of the Knights before Shawn ran away, was nothing special, but Shawn did get in one pinfall: On Owen Hart, who accidentally bumped into Bret and got rolled up by Shawn. Owen had been working in the WWF for years and was kept on the payroll mostly thanks to the influence of his brother, and now Bret wanted to do something bigger with him.

Owen accused Bret of being jealous because Owen had more natural talent than Bret and called Bret selfish for not sharing his success. Bret insisted for weeks that he didn't want to fight his own younger brother, and finally convinced Owen to reconcile and team with him to challenge the Quebecers for the tag titles at Royal Rumble 94. However, Bret's knee was injured during that match, and when he went for the Sharpshooter it gave way and the match was stopped and awarded to the Quebecers. A frustrated Owen, who felt that Bret should have tagged him in, snapped and attacked his brother, which further damaged the leg and set up a feud between them. Both Luger and Bret were entered in the Royal Rumble match itself, which drew high numbers. After eliminating the competition, it was down to those two, but the WWF didn't want to eliminate one of them as a title contender at Wrestlemania, so they had both men hit the floor simultaneously, making the match a draw and producing "co-winners." The fan sentiment was clearly with Bret Hart, however, and that was all the WWF needed to hear. Wrestlemania X was set up with the unique stipulation that a coin toss would decide who got the first shot at Yokozuna, with the eventual WWF champion then facing the other person at the end of the night. Luger won the toss, so he faced Yokozuna first and the winner would meet Bret Hart for the title in the main event. To ensure fairness, Bret Hart had to face brother Owen as "suitable competition" before the main event. The week before the show, the WWF tried to swerve online fans by doing a (never used) TV taping segment where Luger "stole" the WWF title belt from Yokozuna and paraded around with it.

The night began with Bret Hart losing to brother Owen in a

shocking upset (and a ★★★★★ match) as Owen reversed a victory roll for the pin. The big swerve of the night then came, as Luger lost the title match to Yokozuna by DQ, setting up Bret v. Yokozuna for the title in a rematch of Wrestlemania IX, which was the plan all along. Bret regained his title when Yokozuna missed a buttdrop and was pinned. Lex Luger was demoted to the midcard and left for WCW in 1995. Bret spent much of 1994 fighting brother Owen, although behind the scenes they were closer than ever thanks to having the chance to work together everyday. Bret won every rematch from Wrestlemania, and stopped to defend against Diesel at King of the Ring 94 along the way, which led to the last match between the brothers: A cage match at Summerslam 94. Bret won that one after about forty minutes of intense action, which produced the second ★★★★★ match between them that year, a match that was still overshadowed by the Michaels-Ramon ladder match at Wrestlemania X at year-end awards time. And deservedly so, which shows how amazing the ladder match truly was.

Bret's final challenge for the title came in the unlikely form of Mr. Bob Backlund. Bob, who at forty-five years old was making a most unexpected comeback, had "snapped" during a televised title match with Bret Hart earlier in the year and became a raving psychopath. This was in stark contrast to the white-bread, "Howdy Doody" image portrayed by Backlund for decades before the match. He began attacking random WWF officials and wrestlers, locking them all in his crossface-chicken wing submission move and openly claiming that he had never lost the WWF title to the Iron Sheik ten years prior. Backlund finally got another shot at Bret at Survivor Series 94 in a submission match. To win, one wrestler had to make his opponent's cornerman throw in the towel, literally. Bret was represented by the British Bulldog, and Backlund by Owen Hart. At one point in the match, Backlund caught Bret in the crossface, but Bulldog had been knocked unconscious in a skirmish with Owen and was unable to throw in the towel and save Bret. Owen suddenly had a change of heart, begging and pleading with Stu Hart (sitting at ringside with wife Helen) to spare Bret further agony and throw in the towel on his behalf. Although Stu knew what Owen was up to, Helen wasn't so wise to her son's ways, and after enough (fake) tears and pleading from Owen, she grabbed the towel and threw it in, making Bob Backlund the new WWF champion. Owen, of course, immediately hollered with joy and ran away, having cost Bret the title.

After battling to a draw with new WWF champion Diesel at Royal Rumble 95, Bret's career bogged down to helping elevate midcarders and generally wasting his potential. He easily dispatched Bob Backlund in an "I Quit" match at Wrestlemania XI, then got put back into a less-than-inspired feud with Jerry Lawler. Lawler first brought in Japanese star Hakushi (Jinsei Shinzaki) to go after Bret. Bret defeated him at the first *In Your House* show, but was then goaded into a match with Lawler himself, which he lost thanks to Hakushi's interference. Bret destroyed Lawler at *King of the Ring 95* in a "Kiss My Foot" match and Lawler was indeed forced to kiss Bret's foot. Bret was becoming less than thrilled with the WWF's treatment of him, and that continued as Lawler then recruited his dentist, Isaac Yankem (known today as Kane) to go after Bret. Yankem was played by Glen Jacobs, a rookie recruited straight out of Smoky Mountain Wrestling due to his size and speed. Bret won that match by DQ at Summerslam, but then got stuck in a feud with the pirate Jean-Pierre Lafitte and had to get a good match out of him too. He grew more disenchanted with the WWF's insistence on making him sit by the sidelines while Diesel tanked the promotion as champion, and he became vocal about it. The WWF finally capitulated and put the title back on him at Survivor Series 95 with intentions of an eventual Bret v. Shawn match at Wrestlemania.

Bret wasn't happy about being a champion solely so that Shawn could beat him in six months, but he was still the champion. Bret defended the title against the British Bulldog in a gruesomely bloody match at In Your House V (although the company line was that Bret's blood was "accidental," as though anyone ever accidentally cut their forehead open), and then defeated the Undertaker by DQ at Royal Rumble 96 when Diesel prevented a pinfall for the challenger. This made Bret look even weaker (he would have lost without Diesel's interference), and led to a Bret v. Diesel cage match at In Your House VI. Bret's standing was again diminished when the finish saw Undertaker screw Diesel out of the win and essentially hand the title to Bret.

Bret's stay at the top of the WWF limped to its end as he jobbed to Shawn Michaels at Wrestlemania XII and lost the WWF title. He cut a bitter promo on the WWF TV shows following that loss, and refused to put Michaels over and essentially saying "I'll be back." He then took some time off to mull over whether the WWF was where he wanted to spend the rest of his career or if WCW might be worth a shot. So he started entertaining offers from Eric Bischoff and WCW, offers that made him the biggest potential "free agent" signing in wrestling history. In fact, he made a rather flippant "demand" to Bischoff for a ludicrous amount of money, a number that Eric immediately accepted without question. Make no mistake, Bret Hart was now a very hot property, and it would have been a major crowing point for WCW if they had managed to "steal" Kevin Nash, Scott Hall, and Bret within the span of six months. It was no big secret that Vince McMahon was in bad financial shape following the Kevin Nash WWF title experiment, and to lose Bret Hart to rival WCW would be a blow to the ego too big to recover from. So he sucked up his pride and, instead of competing directly with Ted Turner's pocketbook, offered Bret an equal monetary deal, but spread out over twenty years, and with Bret retiring and joining the front office when the deal was over. In October 1996, Bret accepted, and Vince promised him the slot as the number one babyface in the company again and all was well. That lasted all of a week.

By November, with Bret under contract, Vince was already asking Bret to turn heel. Vince's reasoning: As a face, Bret's opponents were limited to essentially Vader or Mankind, while as a heel Bret could draw good money against Undertaker, Shawn Michaels, or

Steve Austin. Given that explanation, Bret agreed and helped to come up with the "Canadian Hero" gimmick for his feud with Steve Austin. To that end, Bret began cultivating a "whiner" image, losing the Royal Rumble due to shenanigans from Steve Austin and complaining about it incessantly afterward. Bret was given a one-day WWF title reign, his fourth, when original choice Steve Austin was injured during the "Final Four" match and couldn't finish. Bret and Austin had a gruesome, intense match at Wrestlemania 13 where Bret officially turned heel and Austin officially turned face, and from there Bret launched the "Canadian hero" gimmick that he had planned. Bret and Austin went to war on Monday Night RAW for the next four months, a feud that served to make Austin look like a convincing badass and Bret like a crybaby. Bret found himself becoming more and more uncomfortable with this portrayal after years of being the "hero" of the story, and Shawn Michaels was now tweaking him every chance he could, trying to provoke a reaction out of him backstage at every opportunity.

By August, Bret was so over as a heel that the WWF had no choice but to put the title back on him, and they did so at Summerslam 97 when Bret defeated Undertaker for the title in a match where Shawn Michaels was the special referee. Bret was becoming increasingly paranoid about Michaels upstaging him in instances exactly like this one, as Michaels hit Undertaker with a chair by accident to cost him the title, thus shifting the heat from the feud onto Shawn v. Undertaker. Bret was then left in the cold, fighting the Patriot for the title while Shawn and Undertaker headlined the next two PPVs. Bret's momentum as lead heel was now evaporating at the hands of Michaels, and then McMahon dropped the bomb on him. In September 1997, Vince approached Bret and told him that the WWF's financial situation was now worse than when Bret had signed the contract, and he would need to defer some of the money promised him. Bret was wary but trusted McMahon. By October, McMahon's story had now changed and he wanted to nearly halve Bret's pay and reimburse him later. Bret refused for obvious reasons, and then a few days later

McMahon simply told him outright that the WWF could no longer
afford the contract and would intentionally breach it. Bret was en-
couraged to visit Eric Bischoff and make whatever deal he wanted,
with the blessing of the WWF.

In essence, Vince had gotten an extra year out of Bret at a reduced rate, and now he wanted to rid himself of him and use Shawn
Michaels as the number one heel. Shawn had defeated Bret's brother-
in-law and partner Davey Boy Smith in England one month prior to
win the European title, which puzzled many people. The title was
generally considered to have been created solely as a trophy of sorts
for Smith, and to actually change the title—and in Smith's home country no less—seemed to have no explanation short of removing the
Hart family from the WWF scene. The plan was now clearly for
Shawn to get the title from Bret (they were scheduled to meet at *Survivor Series 97*), but with an increasingly arrogant Michaels now publicly stating that he wouldn't job to anyone else in the promotion,
Bret's paranoia was seeming more real by the day. The show, as many
of you reading know, was in Montreal, Quebec, Canada.

The legal hassles began immediately. Bret's contract had a "creative control" clause that essentially gave him reasonable control over
his character for 30 days before his termination should he leave the
promotion. That meant the WWF couldn't just tell him to lose to anyone, he had to agree to it. And the last person on earth he would
lose to at that point was Shawn Michaels. Vince attempted a com-
promise: Lose to Michaels in Montreal, regain it a month later, leave
the WWF as champion and give it up on RAW before you go. Bret
responded by noting that he had no guarantee that Michaels would
agree to job the title back to him. Everyone was brought together in
a meeting and Shawn broke down in tears and promised to return
the favor to Bret after Survivor Series. Bret was skeptical, and that was
proven to be a good instinct, because a few days later, Michaels
was up to his old tricks again by taking potshots at Bret's family in
on-screen interviews despite an agreement between them not to do so.

Bret became more torn when Bischoff made him a huge money offer as the deadline for his decision approached. Bret called Vince to ask for some sort of reassurance for his position in the company to convince him to stay, but Vince presented a scenario for Bret's last three months in the company that would weaken his position even further before jobbing him to Steve Austin (which was going to happen to whoever was champion by Wrestlemania, short of Pope John Paul II himself becoming a wrestler and winning the title, so no big deal there). Bret tearfully bid the WWF goodbye and accepted the WCW offer of about $3 million per year. But they still had to get the title off Bret. McMahon was insistent on Bret jobbing to Shawn in Montreal. Bret issued a counteroffer—he would job the title to anyone in the entire company from Vader down to the Brooklyn Brawler anywhere in the United States in the two weeks leading up to the show, and what they did with the title from there was the WWF's business. Vince made a counter-counteroffer: Job to Michaels, in Montreal, or they would sue. Bret made a counter-counter-counteroffer, which involved kissing his nether regions and an argument ensued that lasted well over a day. Finally, after hours of yelling and legal threats, they agreed to a DQ finish for the show and Bret would surrender the title on RAW the next night.

And now the news had broken over the Internet and the Canadian media, and the reaction was immediate: shock and disbelief. WWF Canada tried to lie and cover up the situation, but the truth came out soon enough.* A good chunk of the wrestling fanbase now knew that the Survivor Series would be Bret's farewell match. The WWF played up the "last Shawn vs. Bret match ever" aspect to get

---

*From Dave Meltzer's *Wrestling Observer Newsletter,* November 17, 1997: "November 4, 1997: In response, WWF Canada released a press statement originally totally denying the story, claiming it was simply propaganda being spread by WCW. However, as the word got out, Titan Sports in Connecticut, a few hours later, contradicted that story saying simply that Bret Hart was exploring all his options but not going any further, with the feeling that they wanted to protect the PPV show. Hart wouldn't publicly talk to anyone."

more buys for the show and now the public sniping from both sides was becoming more bitter by the minute. Vince McMahon made a public statement, the famous "WWF Attitude" speech, where he insisted that the intelligence of the fans not be insulted and that his characters were shades of gray, rather than black-or-white "good guys" and "bad guys." The speech was intended to spin the situation to make it sound like Bret was leaving because of the content and direction of the WWF. Bret Hart went on TSN's "Off the Record" talk show and admitted that he had given his thirty-day notice, but didn't say much more. Bret did a house show in Toronto and another in Detroit, two opportunities for the WWF to get him to drop the WWF title before Survivor Series, neither of which was taken. They wanted the title on the line to give the Shawn-Bret maximum impact.

If Bret's paranoia had been bad before, he was positively off the charts now. Other wrestlers began giving him ominous warnings about the "old days," back when Lou Thesz used to have to handle himself in real-life fight situations when a scenario with a promoter turned ugly. Bret couldn't quite bring himself to admit the possibility, but just to be on the safe side he went to the referee of the match—Earl Hebner—and asked for his personal word of honor that he would not screw Bret over and double-cross him. Earl made that promise, going so far as to swear on his kids' lives that he wouldn't double-cross Hart. Bret's fear was that if Vince couldn't convince Bret to lose the title in a worked match, it would turn into a real one and he'd get the title off him that way.

The WWF brain trust and Shawn Michaels had a secret meeting that day, twenty-four hours before the Survivor Series, and all emerged looking unhappy with what had been discussed. Bret was never informed of the meeting. At *Survivor Series*, Bret and Shawn were put in opposite sides of the dressing room with armed guards. Thankfully they weren't needed as both acted like professionals in discussing the match. Bret had no idea what the finish would be, thinking only in vague terms of a DQ. Shawn has since sworn up and down that he didn't know what the finish would be. After he found Jesus, he admitted he had lied about his role in the whole thing and in fact was in on it from the beginning. By a weird quirk of fate, the camera crew for the documentary "Wrestling with Shadows" just happened to be backstage filming at the time so that everything that went down was captured for posterity.

Bret and Shawn had a very good match that night, giving the fans a wild brawl for about thirteen minutes before moving into the ring for the actual match. Vince McMahon, the usual announcer for the WWF PPVs, was strangely absent from his position that night, a position to which he has never returned. Shawn made sure to pick his nose with the Canadian flag to solidify himself as a heel for the Canadian crowd. As they fought back into the ring, Vince himself made his way back to ringside to watch and many other WWF personnel joined him. Security began moving into position. Had Bret noticed these things, he might have saved himself, but he didn't. As the match neared what Bret thought was the scheduled finish, referee Hebner was bumped and knocked unconscious. Shawn put Bret in his own finisher—the Sharpshooter. Then everything went weird.

At this point, a second referee, Mike Ciota, was supposed to come in and take over, followed by the other Hart Foundation members (Owen and Bulldog in this case), who would cause the DQ loss for Bret. Instead, Earl Hebner miraculously recovered and jumped back into position. Backstage, Ciota and the Harts immediately panicked, realizing what was about to happen. They were prevented from going anywhere by security, however. Bret Hart was in a submission move, his own move, and Earl Hebner was now in position to check for the submission. None came, but Vince McMahon, suddenly moving from his position at ringside, jabbed the timekeeper in the ribs and yelled at him to "Ring the bell, ring the fucking bell" as Earl called for the submission. Bret continued the match for a few seconds, unaware of what had just happened, and reversed the move as planned. But the bell had rung and Shawn's music was playing, and now it sunk in. He had been double-crossed. Shawn was hastily given the title belt and herded to the dressing room, and Earl Hebner followed and was put into a taxi bound for the hotel at top speed to escape Bret if need be. Bret, attempting to maintain his dignity, spat on Vince McMahon, drew the "WCW" letters in the air with his finger, and then lost all semblance of control and smashed several ringside monitors and furniture. Back in the dressing room, Vince apologized and Bret punched his lights out with one shot to the face. The general feeling in the locker room was that they wanted to do exactly the same thing, but Vince was out cold so they didn't have to. The WWF locker room came the closest it ever has to completely rebelling against McMahon that night, with many wrestlers vowing not to work RAW the next day in Ottawa. In the end, cooler heads prevailed, and only Owen Hart, British Bulldog, and Mankind missed the show in protest. Mankind was only barely important enough to the company to skip the show and avoid being fired outright. Things looked bleak Monday night and the WWF put on a dreary show that annoyed the already upset Canadian crowd even further. People speculated that this was rock bottom for the WWF and WCW would now crush them for good.

When the ratings came in the next day they were up a full point from the week before due to the controversy and intrigue of the Survivor Series. Everyone assumed that they would drop again soon enough but they didn't, because the WWF was putting on a strong product at that point and all they had needed was a jumpstart to get some extra viewers hooked on it. Shawn Michaels, who had promised Bret the night before that he had no part in the screwjob, had also guaranteed that he would never in a million years accept the WWF title under those circumstances and would never in a million years trash Bret after the fact. And on that fateful show, Shawn proceeded to formally accept the WWF title and trash Bret after the fact. Bret Hart was now, as far as the WWF was concerned, dead and buried.

Vince McMahon, the mild-mannered play-by-play announcer was dead. Mr. McMahon the evil owner was born. Whereas Bret was bound for three years of misuse, injuries, and political problems with the nWo, Vince came out about a billion dollars ahead on the whole deal when his character met up with Steve Austin again in December 1997 and kicked off the biggest-drawing feud in the history of wrestling. And Bret was bound for WCW, the one place he never wanted to end up. Although the WWF was a disaster for a few weeks after Bret's departure and everyone assumed that this would be the crushing blow in WCW's favor, really there were other factors working against WCW. The first was that Bret Hart really never wanted to be in WCW and didn't know how to handle the strange, hyper-political atmosphere created there. Eric Bischoff blames Bret more directly for having a lack of passion and commitment, but the handling of him was very strange, to say the least. Bischoff had brought Bret into the company with promises of making him into the biggest star in the world and running Canada, but almost immediately upon his entrance into the company the backstabbing and second-guessing began. He was used as a plot device in the big Sting v. Hulk Hogan main event of *Starrcade 97*, which made him look useless right out of the gate. The story here is typical WCW: They spent more than a year building up Sting as the mysterious challenger to the evil Hollywood Hulk Hogan's WCW World title, never speaking and never doing anything in the ring. By the time the match was finally signed fans were absolutely rabid to see Hogan get what was coming to him and Sting get the title after months of chasing him down. However, the match was supposed to have Hogan pinning Sting while evil referee Nick Patrick gave a very fast count, which would set up Bret coming out and restarting the match so that what happened to him in Montreal would be avenged. What happened instead was that Hogan decided that he wasn't going to lose to Sting, and bribed Nick Patrick into counting at regular speed when the time came. So now Sting looks like a chump for losing the big match cleanly, and then

Bret Hart comes out and looks like a whiner for complaining about what was clearly a fair fight. End result: Hogan gets the title back a few months later and everyone else disappears off the radar.

After that debacle, Bret's first real program was against Ric Flair, who he had never really gotten a chance to work with in the WWF outside of winning his first WWF World title from him. So they were matched up against each other on a nothing show called *Souled Out 98*, which was literally promoted for less than a week on WCW's TV shows and was expected to lose money because of the noninvolvement of the almighty Hulk Hogan and Sting. To everyone's shock, mainly WCW's, Bret and Flair managed to draw some pretty good numbers as the main event, and people still liked Flair enough to care about him. So with no notice given to either guy, they were first teamed up to end that feud, and then that team was abruptly dropped a week later as well. For all of Bischoff's big talk before bringing him in, no one in the company wanted Bret Hart to succeed, and they didn't know what to do with him anyway.

Bret's most well-known stab at becoming a star in WCW came midway through 1998, when WCW finally ran a show in Toronto, guaranteeing a huge babyface reaction for Bret. First of all they wanted to make him a heel, because no one would be expecting that. Then Bret pitched an idea that he got from watching Clint Eastwood movies: He would call out WCW World champion Goldberg while wearing a Maple Leafs sweater, and Goldberg would then charge into the ring and hit him with his deadly finishing move, the spear. However, after delivering the move, Goldberg would crumple into a heap and Bret would be unscathed, revealing instead a piece of metal under his sweater. Well, this turned into a huge deal backstage, as Bischoff was paranoid about showing Goldberg to be weak in any way, and he also wanted to get Hogan involved, pitching a replacement idea where Hogan would then come out and turn on Bret after pretending to be his friend. This of course would make no sense because Bret and Hogan weren't going to be wrestling each other at any point, but

Bischoff essentially just felt that Hogan had to get involved some-how and made Bret ask Hogan for permission to go ahead without using him. In the end, there was never any big Bret Hart v. Gold-berg match to settle things, and he continued aimlessly drifting through WCW for the rest of 1998.

The problem with Bret in WCW for most of the way was that he was too big of a star to let go, but he was not perceived as a big enough star to hang with the guys on top like Hogan and Sting. Mostly what he was used for was making new stars out of guys like Booker T and Goldberg, and even that would have been fine with Bret had they let him do more than a week's worth of build to any of it. By 1999, Bret was in and out of the promotion with injuries, and then his life hit rock bottom with the death of Owen Hart. He took a leave of absence from the promotion, unsure whether his ca-reer would continue. During that time off Eric Bischoff was fired as President of WCW, which at least freed up one obstacle barring Bret's ascent to the top again. During that time off, Vince McMahon asked Bret for a one-on-one meeting in a public place so they could dis-cuss burying the hatchet and giving Bret control of his own video-tape library again, something that Bret had been lobbying for in his last days as a part of the WWF in 1997. In fact, Vince had no inten-tion of following through on any of the promises made, and was merely trying to win Bret over so that the lawsuit brought on in the wake of the Owen Hart death would be dropped.

Bret did return to WCW in October 1999 and wrestled in a clas-sic match against Chris Benoit that was billed as a tribute to Owen Hart. It would be the last classic match of Bret's career, as he won the match despite repeatedly asking to lose and thus make a star out of Benoit, but the new WCW regime had bigger plans for Bret. He fi-nally won the WCW World title by defeating Benoit in a rematch that was the finals of a long and agonizing (for the fans) tournament that concluded at *Mayhem 99* in Toronto. Bret was seemingly on top, but it was really a sad afterthought in his once great career. He finally got his feud with Goldberg kickstarted for real and wrestled him for the title in the main event of *Starrcade 99,* but during the course of the match the stiff and inexperienced Goldberg kicked Bret in the head too hard, giving Bret an instant concussion and actually breaking a hole in his skull as a result. Bret continued to work for a few weeks afterward but never received any support from WCW outside of some Advil, and he finally had to vacate the title and retire after a match with Terry Funk. He had trouble functioning on a day-to-day basis as a result of his injuries, and he called it quits. Later Bret officially retired to end his contract with WCW in October 2000 and at least got to go out as World champion.

His life hit bottom in June 2002, when he was riding his bike and suffered a stroke from his years of accumulated injuries, which propelled him over the handlebars and caused him to land on the back of his head. He suffered partial paralysis as a result of the accident and it took years for him to recover enough to truly get his life back in order again. That being said, Bret escaped wrestling in time to make it out alive and he's one of the few who retired with his financial future secure. His career was clearly on the downslide by the time he got to WCW, and had he stayed with the sinking ship he would have become just another face in the endless parade of ex-WCW losers trying to crawl to the WWF for a job when the company was sold to Vince McMahon. The way he went out, he was able to leave on top of the promotion and holding their title, thus guaranteeing himself status as a legend instead of a has been. He has since mostly mended his fences with Vince McMahon over the Montreal incident, and was inducted into the WWE Hall of Fame in 2006, something that no one in their right mind would have guessed just five years before.

The real tragedy for Bret is that his personal life fell apart and that after years of mentoring younger wrestlers, he had to helplessly watch the people he cared about die while he lived on. His wife left him after a tumultuous marriage and four children, although Bret is very upfront about his infidelities in the course of his autobiography. But he also makes no bones about the fact that it was the nature of the business and his years on the road that tore them apart. He always seemed to believe himself to be bigger than the business, a guy who could have changed things, and I think that turning into the helpless victim of Vince McMahon and an even more helpless victim of a stroke left him without the one thing he craved the most: Control over his own destiny. Although the drugs and partying may not have gotten him in the end, he was done in by something even more powerful—the lure of his own fame.

OWEN HART

The Show Must Go On

—Queen

On May 23, 1999, my friends were having their usual congregation at my apartment and watching the WWF's latest pay-per-view offering called *Over the Edge*. I was at work that night, bummed about missing a show that looked pretty good but otherwise not thinking much about it. That all changed when I walked in and my roommate somberly announced "Owen Hart is dead. He died in the ring." My first thought was that this had to be a really sick joke on his part, because he was known for that sort of thing in the past. But once we had established that, in fact, he was telling the truth and Owen really had plunged to his death on live TV, I was pretty sure it was going to be one of those moments. For me, it was the moment when everything changed as far as my wrestling fandom went. Before, I had been a blissfully ignorant watcher of our so-called sport, generally upset at the WWF for being over-the-top and destroying the livelihoods of other promoters but not taking it personally. Now my favorite wrestler in the world was dead, and they couldn't even stop the fucking show. Although my writing career was just beginning at that point, people have since told me that I got a lot more bitter and hateful toward the WWF from then on, and they're probably right. For a long time afterward, I was ashamed to call myself a fan of any business that would let something like that happen to the person who brought such happiness to me through his performance. The WWF went on to make billions of dollars more despite Owen's death, and Owen's family ended up self-destructing. Truly there is no justice, and even now it hurts to write about it.

But the show must go on, or so I've been told by Vince McMahon.

Our story begins on May 7, 1965, with the birth of the youngest of the Hart brothers, Owen. It is the same story you hear all too often in wrestling families: Someone seems like they're going to be the one to transcend the business and become something bigger than it, but he gets sucked in anyway. I guess you could say Owen was the Michael Corleone of the Hart family. He was a talented amateur wrestler, living out Stu's dream of reaching the Olympics in wrestling, but what he really wanted to do was teach. Or be a firefighter. Anything to avoid the same world of wrestling that overtook all his brothers and sisters. And yet there he was at age sixteen, wrestling under a mask to fill vacant positions on Stampede shows while studying Japanese tapes. Owen was actually a very good amateur wrestler, attending the University of Calgary on a wrestling scholarship while working toward his teaching degree, but by 1986 the wrestling program was shut down and Owen was forced to turn pro, debuting for his father's promotion and becoming an instant sensation. Whereas Bret was the solid mat technician and Bruce was, well, whatever he booked himself to be, Owen was clearly the Hart brother for the next generation. Watching the shows as a teenager and seeing Owen backflip into the ring, something only done in Mexico and Japan up until that point, would set the stage for a high-flying exhibition that promised something new and different for the territory. He would have matches with Viet Cong Express #1 (the future Japanese legend Hiro Hase) that were years ahead of their time. But more than that, Owen exuded the true babyface persona at that young age. He was truly a guy who women in the audience fawned over and, much like Ricky

Morton before him, he was able to play on their sympathies and draw huge heat by being the pretty young thing who the ugly heels beat on before he made the big comeback.

One girl in the audience who definitely fawned over his baby face was Martha Patterson, who went from high school sweetheart to wife and remained with him for the rest of his life. Martha always hated wrestling and actively discouraged him from pursuing it as a career, but in the end having all his brothers in the business was just too much to escape and he was in. One thing he did differently, however, was manage his finances. Whereas others partied away their money, Owen's salary was added to a nest egg like clockwork, which began a legend of his cheapness that was rivaled only by that of his in-ring prowess. Many of the "boys" would razz him about his frugal ways over the years, but then many of those same boys would end up having to work retail jobs to pay the bills after the fame had departed.

Owen was money for Stampede as he quickly captured the tag team titles with brother-in-law Ben Bassarab, and then simultaneously held the mid-heavyweight title and the North American heavyweight title. He carryied the promotion on his back in its dying years. Some of my fondest memories of the Stampede promotion came from this doomed era, with Owen and Mike "Makhan Singh" Shaw putting on ★★★★ matches night after night with the 400-pound Singh an unlikely opponent to keep up with the acrobatics of Owen. But because you weren't expecting that kind of performance out of the heel was what made them such great matches, and thus it was all the more satisfying when Owen got the big win in the end. But the promotion clearly was dying, and once the evil Makhan Singh won the title for good and there were no more heroic comebacks to be made, there was really only one destination after that: The World Wrestling Federation.

Still stuck in the cartoon world of the '80s but not drawing the same audience, the WWF of 1989 was a much different place. With

Bret Hart only known as a tag-team wrestler at that point, Owen didn't have a "name" to draw on and needed a gimmick. Long a fan of Japanese masked wrestlers and wanting to mimic something in the Tiger Mask vein, he started out as the American Eagle before a series of Vince's famous changes of heart left him as the Blue Blazer. Although he had good matches, it was still the time of larger-than-life musclemen like Ultimate Warrior and Hulk Hogan, and someone as small as Owen was doomed from the start. That gimmick initially went nowhere, although it gained much more infamy in later years.

After a very short stint in the WCW as little more than a trivia note (Trivia: What was the name of the team that Owen and Brian Pillman formed during their one match together before Owen left again? "Wings."), Owen resurfaced in the WWF in 1991 with Bret becoming a pretty big singles star. This time he was given a small push as part of The New Foundation with brother-in-law Jim Neidhart, and they played off the original Hart Foundation team except with baggy tights and now courting to the kiddie crowd that the WWF was trying to win back. When that went over like a fart in church, the team was reworked with Koko B Ware replacing Jim Neidhart, and the pants got even puffier as the team became High Energy. Amazingly, this tactic didn't work either, and Owen was repackaged yet again as a singles wrestler dubbed "The Rocket" and doing bland midcard matches. Finally, by 1993, he was ready to give up the WWF again and try his luck elsewhere, but Bret talked the promotion into giving Owen one more shot with the old "family feud" angle. According to an interview with Bret in 2000, the original idea was a feud with Bruce Hart of all people, which would lead to the heel-ified Bruce losing and then retiring to become a fireman. Bret turned down this idea and wanted Owen for the slot instead, because Owen and Bret were always the closest of the brothers and according to Bret, "Bruce would have killed the heat."

The really sad thing about that feud is that for a short while, Bret and Owen had to play a tag team in order to build up the heel turn for Owen. I say this is sad because the matches were so ridiculously good and they had such a natural presence as a team that it only emphasized how great they could have been had they worked as a team on a full-time basis. As it was, even with their shortened tenure they managed to produce one all-time classic tag team match against the Steiner Brothers that only exists on a WWF home video release called *Wrestlefest 94* and has long been a hot commodity among tape-trading enthusiasts. Who knows what the team would have produced had it been allowed to proceed along a more drawn-out breakup?

Regardless, the seeds were sown at *Survivor Series 1993* when Bret teamed up with Owen and fellow Hart brothers Bruce and Keith for a one-shot deal against Shawn Michaels and his "knights": Greg Valentine, Jeff Gaylord, and Barry Horowitz who worked under masks. The match was originally supposed to feature Jerry "The King" Lawler in the lead heel role (which would have made the "knights" much more meaningful as a gimmick), but Lawler was busy fighting a statutory rape charge (he was later acquitted) and Shawn Michaels had to step in. At this point, Bret and Shawn had none of the conflict in real life that they would later become famous for. The match was simply the means to an end, and the Harts picked off the heels one-by-one, until Shawn was the only wrestler left on the heel team. He got a fluke pinfall on Owen Hart and then ran out on the match. The setup then became that Owen was bitter because he wasn't good enough in Bret's eyes, and he wanted a match. Standard stuff, but it worked well despite Owen's track record for playing a blue-eyed babyface and not the sniveling heel he would become more famous for. When they finally had their match six months later at *Wrestlemania X*, it was one hell of a match. They opened the show with Bret insisting on putting his brother over, and it was here that Owen's whiny little brat persona was born. Bret's explanation, again from an interview in 2000, is that if Bret had simply beat up his little brother people would inevitably start cheering for Owen, because who wants to see the big star acting like a bully? But by keeping Owen an irri-

tating little jerk, people are more concerned with seeing him "get
his" than with worrying about who's bigger.

Owen's push continued through 1994 as he won the second annual *King of the Ring* tournament on PPV by defeating Razor Ramon
in the finals, and thus proclaimed himself "The King of Harts" as
his next gimmick. Owen went through a lot of gimmicks over his
WWF career, I should note. Owen was pushed as the number one
contender to Bret's newly won WWF title for the first half of 1994,
although their house show matches were generally disappointing due
to Bret's tendency to pay less attention to nontelevised matches and
do only what was absolutely necessary rather than making an extra
effort. That feud culminated in a cage match at *Summerslam 94* that
I rated ★★★★★ and it generally stands as the best example of the
"escape to win" style of cage match that featured an athletic exhibition by both men and lots of really cool reversals of fortune and attempts to get out of the cage. By this time Owen was basically a
nonfactor in the World title scene and floated around the tag team
ranks for the rest of the year with former partner Jim Neidhart, until
Neidhart's firing led to Owen's next big push. After The New Foundation were eliminated from a tournament for the vacant tag team titles
in early 1995, Owen began complaining (as per usual for his character) about unfair conditions and demanded a rematch with eventual champions The Smoking Gunns with a partner of his choosing.
That partner turned out to be Yokozuna, and suddenly Owen had
his first major championship and a revival of both his and Yokozuna's
careers. Yokozuna's limited mobility and failing health meant that
their reign was fairly short and notable for only the most ridiculous
example of bait-and-switch in decades that was perpetrated by Vince
McMahon on the *In Your House III* show. The WWF promoted a match
between the tag champs and WWF champion Diesel, who was teamed
with Intercontinental champion Shawn Michaels. The stipulation was
that whoever scored the pinfall got the title of whoever they pinned.
In fact, advertising for the event literally guaranteed a title change

that night, but you obviously don't understand the genius of Vince McMahon, because what we got instead was a faked "no-show" by Owen Hart with British Bulldog subbing for him. So Shawn & Diesel won the match (by pinning Owen Hart, who ran into the match at the last minute), and the titles were returned the next night because Owen wasn't legally in the match. Take that, paying customers!

After dropping the titles back to the Gunns, Owen floated around the midcard as a member of Jim Cornette's stable before getting back into the title picture in September 1996 and winning the tag titles again with brother-in-law British Bulldog. However, it wasn't until 1997 that their title reign would mean anything, although it meant something huge—namely, the Hart Foundation. After months of teasing a breakup between the brothers-in-law, which culminated with Bulldog defeating Owen in the finals of a tournament for the newly created European title in a match that was one of the best of the 90s, Owen and Bulldog had one last match to settle the score for good. Still tag team champions, they battled on the March 31, 1997 edition of Monday Night RAW, a show that was beginning to build momentum after more than a year of humiliating losses to Nitro in the ratings. After another classic match, with both men ready to throw out the proverbial rulebook and seemingly split for good, Bret Hart stopped them in mid-fight and reunited his family in a tearful scene. The great thing is that Bret had spent the previous week insulting the USA and what would normally be a heartfelt and emotional moment turned all three into the biggest villains in the WWF . . . but only in the U.S. In Canada and the rest of the world, they were the heroes that they proclaimed themselves to be. It was a truly inspired type of storyline, one that had never really been seen in the modern era of wrestling. Playing off unlikely hero Steve Austin as their foil, the Hart Foundation angle revived business for the WWF in 1997 and led to Owen winning the Intercontinental title in April, his first singles championship in the WWF.

His showdown with Steve Austin at *Summerslam 97* was historic for another reason besides their already-heated rivalry on-screen. The finish of the match was supposed to see Owen delivering three pile-drivers to Austin, only to have Austin miraculously kick out and fire back with his patented Stone Cold Stunner to win the match and the title. Instead, Owen hit the first piledriver, and accidentally drove Austin's head into the mat for real in the process, which left the Rattle-snake paralyzed in the ring and the finish in shambles. Owen man-aged to improvise an ending where he argued with the referee and essentially fell backward to pin himself, but how Austin even man-aged to get up off the mat long enough to execute that is a mystery in itself. In fact, Austin's doctors said that he had "the neck of an 80-year-old man" and it was a shock that he was able to perform as well as he had even before that match. When he returned in No-vember—far too soon to be healthy—it was obvious that the pro-motion was going to be built around only one person: Steve Austin. The entire main event direction changed to suit his new low-impact ring style and emphasizing a more storytelling approach. Whereas before people would suplex each other and hit each other with chairs to gain the crowd's attention, Austin's injury meant that he would often brawl with his opponent into the crowd and substitute walk-ing for wrestling. The change was surprisingly effective and created the homogenized style that came to be known as "Main Event Style" among the websites and newsletters.

However, whereas Austin's star was rising, Owen's was falling. Being the guy who nearly killed the biggest star in the company was bad enough to have hanging over his head (and Austin was rumored to want Owen nowhere near him in the main event as a result), but when Montreal came and went and Owen was the last guy from the Hart family left in the WWF, things went from bad to worse for him. Not only was he a political enemy of Steve Austin, but he was now on the bad side of Shawn Michaels as well, which left him with no allies on either side of the hottest acts in wrestling at that point. While Austin v. Michaels headlined *Wrestlemania XIV* and drew millions of dollars for the company, Owen was relegated to silly feuds against Shawn's lackey HHH and then got put with the all-black Nation of Domination as a heel. Whereas Bret's departure should have turned Owen into the hottest babyface in the company by seeking revenge for his brother, he was reduced to a comedy act and doing jobs for Ken Shamrock to try and make him into a wrestling star. It didn't work.

But I can't mention the phrase "comedy act" without coming back to the Blue Blazer. Owen's final push came in 1999 when he was doing nothing in the midcard and stuck with fellow driftwood club member Jeff Jarrett as the tag team champions. Sounds fine, but they were really just background noise for the real star of the team, Debra McMichael. She'd strip while they cheated to win, and it was starting to bother Owen. With young kids at home, he had long been an outspoken family man, and here he was being asked to be a part of a fairly risqué act. Although everyone in wrestling says they'll retire in two years and become a motivational speaker, or teacher, or bricklayer, or whatever, Owen's wife Martha swore up and down in her biography of Owen that he really, really meant it, for honest. So we'll take her at her word and assume that Owen really did want to get out of the business in two years and finish his teaching degree. I don't believe it, but I'll play along for the sake of argument. In my own opinion, in case you're wondering, Owen would have kept coming back as long as Vince waved one more paycheck and push under his nose, because he was addicted to the business and denying it would be pointless. At any rate, Owen wanted out and Vince took it personally. So he offered Owen a new storyline once Owen & Jarrett had dropped the tag titles to the oddball team of Kane & X-Pac: In order to split up the team, Debra would hit on Owen, and he would "cheat on his wife" with her and cause jealousy with Jeff Jarrett. This storyline was a total no-go as far as Owen was concerned, so Vince pitched an alternative: Go back to being the Blue Blazer, but take the superhero act over the top and become the crusader for morality in an immoral world. This idea was obviously a shot at groups like the Parent's Television Council (PTC) that decried the low morals of his programming, but it was also a humiliating swipe at Owen and his decision to stand up for what he believed in. But Owen was already on shaky ground, so he went along with it because he was promised another run as Intercontinental champion if he played along.

So the Blue Blazer, who wasn't Owen Hart according to his interviews, began appearing on TV and demanding that the WWF clean up their act, which naturally led him into a conflict with Intercontinental champion The Godfather, who pimped hoes nationwide and ran a real-life strip club in Las Vegas on the side. A match was signed for the *Over the Edge* PPV in May 1999, and Vince suggested that Owen rappel from the ceiling like Shawn Michaels had done at *Wrestlemania XII*, but with a twist: He'd get "caught up" in his ropes and fall to the mat like a bumbling moron. Owen was always terrified of heights, but because the stunt had been pulled off for years in WCW with Sting and with Shawn Michaels in the WWF, he assumed that everything was under control. It was naturally Vince's plan to again mock the forces of wrestling conspiring against him, namely guys like Sting who dared to draw money against him by appearing to be a real-life superhero and descending from the ceiling. They tested it with a strong nylon rope and a mountain-climbing carabiner, but Vince wanted something with a quick release. Owen had protested enough times that he couldn't afford to do it again and agreed to go along with the new plan.

On May 23, 1999, before the third match of the PPV, Owen sneaked into the rafters wearing workman's coveralls over his humiliating Blazer costume. The crowd saw a pre-taped promo on the TitanTron that was supposed to signal his descent, but instead of a smooth fall from the ceiling, the live crowd was instead shocked to hear Owen screaming as he fell at forty-five miles an hour and crashed in an instant into the top turnbuckle. His neck was instantly broken and fans at ringside later described it like a "crash test dummy" hitting the ring. The cameras instantly started shooting the arena instead of the ring, and everyone went into panic mode. Jim Ross made history by using the first instance of "The Owen Voice," as he informed the audience that "This is not part of the entertainment portion of the show. This is as real as real can get," in a hushed tone that would later be duplicated for faked injuries and getting someone over as a bad-ass. Jerry Lawler rushed into the ring to try and help as Owen turned purple. They were using an ambulance for a pre-taped skit with Vince McMahon before the show, and it was hurriedly called back to the arena as paramedics worked on Owen, far too late to do anything to save him. Nothing was mentioned to the crowd as his body was taken from the ring, and the matches continued as though it was just another night of action in the World Wrestling Federation. Most sickeningly, HHH and Rock engaged in a "casket match," complete with pre-taped video of Rock emerging from the casket covered in blood, and later in the night a guy named The Undertaker won the WWF World title from Steve Austin. Later in the show, Jim Ross announced that Owen Hart was dead. People in the arena were never informed.

So why did the show have to continue? Think about this: If you're watching a baseball game and one of the players suddenly drops dead from a horrible accident, do they force everyone else to finish the game? Hell, they don't even play in the *rain* most of the time. If one of the actors drops dead during a play on Broadway, do they finish the show? Of course not, because it's a ludicrous suggestion. Only a company as callous and cold-hearted as the WWF would even suggest something like "Owen would have wanted it that way." Given the strife that followed in the Hart family, it's safe to say that no one in his own family would have known what he wanted at the best of times. Although Vince later protested that the show had to continue so that they could call the Hart family and inform them of the accident, the only person that got a call that night was Martha, and even then Vince was evasive with her, telling her only that Owen was "hurt." The family was devastated, to say the least, and it was the beginning of the end for the Hart family dynasty. Stu was so shaken up he could barely give interviews on the subject, which showed his growing dementia. But he always made sure to talk about how proud he was of Owen. However, soon after the goodwill and prayers came the strife. Davey Boy Smith turned on the family, publicly siding with Vince and the WWF as he hoped for a job. Martha Hart was of course on the other side of things, declaring at the funeral that "There will be a day of reckoning" for Vince and the WWF. The sides were being drawn.

Martha fired the first shot, suing the WWF for negligence and looking to collect hundreds of millions as a result. During the proceedings leading up to the lawsuit, it was revealed that Vince had used a private contractor to set up the rigging, and that the actual quick-release clasp was intended for use on a sailboat and required only six pounds of pressure to release. The WWF countersued for breach of Owen's contract, claiming that because Martha was suing them in Missouri instead of Connecticut it was in violation of his contract. Furthermore, Vince went to Stu Hart directly with an offer of $33 million, no strings attached, to drop any lawsuits and call it even. Stu and Bruce Hart both wanted to accept, but Martha instead asked him to sign away his legal rights and join her own lawsuit instead. Poor Stu didn't want to break up the family and went with Martha's side, although had he known what would follow I'm sure he wouldn't have bothered.

Now the battle began, with Martha, Bret, and Keith on one side wanting to hold Vince accountable for his actions more than the money involved. On the other side, Bruce, Bulldog, and Diana Hart were all trying to stay on Vince's good side and get work again and wanted to accept whatever offer the WWF made. It got ugly. Really ugly. Davey Boy signed with the WWF again in 1999 and Bret penned an infamous column in the *Calgary Sun* where he talked about "dogs rolling around in their own feces and loving every minute of it" in response. Bruce Hart dragged his father onto Monday Night RAW in 2001, long after Stu had much of a clue what was happening around him, so that he could be seen on TV with the WWF and hopefully kickstart his failed attempt to restart Stampede Wrestling. Martha got increasingly crazed in her media appearances, going from a grieving widow to a woman with a seemingly insatiable need to grind an axe with her enemies. Bret's marriage fell apart, as did Bruce's. The family gatherings at Hart House turned into screaming matches, with Stu and Helen caught in the middle. Martha and the family finally accepted a settlement for $18 million when all was said and done, and all it cost them was the total destruction of the family.

And really, that's the saddest part of the whole thing. Worse than the wrestlers who died from drugs, or killed themselves, or ended up crippled, it's the effect on those around them that hurts the most. Not only was Owen dead, but the petty squabbling over the WWF's money tore apart the closest thing that Canada had to a royal family. Did any of it ever get an answer as to why Owen had to die? No. Was anyone happy in the end? Doubtful. But that's wrestling for you—a cold, callous, heartless business that not only sucks the life out of the people involved but the innocent bystanders around them as well. I think the worst thing about the whole situation is that there was no easy answer. Yes, Vince is a money-driven jerk at times, but really it was a freak accident that killed Owen. Blaming Vince wasn't going to bring Owen back, and obviously no amount of money was going to make Martha happy again. Unfortunately, fate is just as cold and callous as wrestling is, sometimes more.

THE VON ERICHS

As long as we're on the subject of death and drugs and pro wrestling riches-to-rags stories, I guess we might as well stop and talk about the strangest one of them all: the Von Erich family.

If Stu Hart and his motley crew of wrestling sons was the closest thing to royalty in Calgary, then Fritz Von Erich and his wrestling sons were Texas royalty in much the same way. In fact, the similarities are striking, starting with the fact that Stu Hart trained Fritz. And much like Stu, Fritz had a vision for his wrestling promotion being the outlet to make huge stars of his sons. And for a while, it worked, more so with Fritz than Stu. To get there, both men were ruthless in their expectations of greatness from their sons, although Stu was more physically abusive whereas Fritz just pushed his boys beyond any reasonable measure of what could be expected from a normal human being. It's debatable which parenting method was worse, although in the end Fritz lost all his sons but one, whereas Stu got off fairly easy with only Owen dying as a result of his dream.

Jack Adkisson, the man who would later be known as Fritz Von Erich, was about as foreign as every other foreigner in wrestling back in the old days. In other words, he was from Dallas, Texas, and was a football star in college before moving to the Edmonton Eskimos of the Canadian Football League in 1953. It was there that he met Stu Hart, and Stu had already become established as a promoter with a soft spot for football players. He enjoyed molding them into wrestlers and using them as part of his Klondike Wrestling promotion, which would later become Stampede Wrestling in the '70s. With his size and imposing grip, Jack was a natural to play a fearsome, goose-stepping Nazi in the heyday of the Cold War, and he was reborn as Fritz Von Erich, master of the dreaded Iron Claw. Whether or not he invented the move is debatable, but there's no shortage of wrestlers to credit him with introducing them to the move. Fritz was an immediate superstar in Klondike Wrestling and soon migrated to St. Louis to expand his reputation. And because of a victory over the legendary Antonio Inoki in the U.S., Fritz became a headliner around the country and even in Japan.

Although Fritz was considered one of the biggest draws in the U.S. and also one of the best wrestlers, he was never able to get the NWA World title because of the perception that he was a "gimmick wrestler," rather than someone like Lou Thesz who wrestled under his real name and wasn't pretending to be another nationality. This notion may sound laughable today in a time when you can't even get a minor title without being a dancing sumo wrestler or transvestite ninja assassin or whatever stupid idea sells tickets, but in the '60s and '70s people still took the NWA World title seriously. Instead, Fritz ended up as the president of the NWA while running his own small promotion out of Texas. And with his power in the industry cemented, Fritz had a revelation. While driving home from a sermon in 1974, Fritz claimed that he heard a "divine voice," which made him open his bible to Psalms 23:

> The LORD [is] my shepherd; I shall not want.
> He maketh me to lie down in green pastures:
> He leadeth me beside the still waters.
> He restoreth my soul:
> He leadeth me in the paths of righteousness for his
>   name's sake.
> Yea, though I walk through the valley of the shadow
>   of Death,

> I will fear no evil: for thou [art] with me; thy rod and
>   thy staff they comfort me.
> Thou preparest a table before me in the presence of
>   mine enemies:
> thou anointest my head with oil; my cup runneth
>   over.
> Surely goodness and mercy shall follow me all the
>   days of my life:
> and I will dwell in the house of the LORD for ever.*

From this he also took the meaning to be an all-American family of boys who could save wrestling and present a strong Christian ethic to the world. Sadly, it ended up totally the opposite for him. His idea started strong as his newly named World Class Championship Wrestling (WCCW) started up in 1981 and was broadcast on local Christian broadcasting stations, which loved the wholesome image being put forth by his sons David, Kevin, and Kerry. David was a tall and lanky kid who hardly looked older than 18 but was already becoming a major star in the sport. He was considered on the fast track to win the NWA World title, and the World Class promotion was built around him and his chase of that title. A falling out with Fritz actually sent David to Florida for a short time in 1982, where he worked as a heel under the tutelage of Dory Funk Jr., and became an even bigger star in the process. The paperwork with the NWA was more or less already done and he had been voted in as champion at the beginning of 1984, when a trip to Japan resulted in his shocking and unexpected death on February 10, 1984. To this day conspiracy theories abound about the death, with the Von Erich family claiming that it was caused by an intestinal infection from bad sushi causing a heart attack and everyone else calling it a drug overdose. It was the first time that the territory would be rocked by the

*King James Bible version

death of a Von Erich, but certainly not the last. And in fact his death
marked the first ever Dead Wrestler Tribute Show, an edition of WCCW
that featured the now-familiar parade of mourning wrestlers and the
even more familiar backlash from the industry when it was claimed
that Fritz was exploiting his son's death for ratings. Perish the thought.

At that point, they hardly needed to exploit death for ratings anyway, because the promotion was on fire thanks to the biggest thing
to hit wrestling in years: The Freebirds v. Von Erichs feud. Although
the territory was solid in the early '80s thanks to the rock star good
looks of the Von Erich boys and the syndication on Christian stations, the company had little else going for it. Local Texas veterans
would pass through and put over the Von Erich kids, but it was obvious that the young audience was only there to see them and not
whoever else would work the undercard. A fresh territory with hot
babyfaces in need of cool heels, with a young and enthusiastic audience, was exactly the formula for success that the young and hungry Freebird team of Michael Hayes, Terry Gordy, and Buddy Roberts
needed. They blew in as babyfaces in 1982, aligned with the Von
Erichs as "friends of David's from Georgia," and achieved minor success as tag team champions there running with that. However, after
Kerry was screwed out of the NWA World title in a storyline against
Ric Flair, they built to a rematch for Christmas 1982 where Kerry
would finally be the one with all the advantages. First, they made it
a cage match to eliminate Flair paying Von Erich rivals to attack him
(as he had been doing leading up to the match). Then fans were
given a chance to vote for a special second referee to make sure that
the officiating wasn't biased, and because the Freebirds had been established as faces, Von Erich ally Michael Hayes won a legitimate
victory in the polls and got the job. Hayes then appointed tag team
partner Terry Gordy the job of guarding the door of the cage, just in
case anyone tried to rush in.

Earlier in the show, the Freebirds won the first ever World Class
World Six-Man titles by defeating Mike Sharpe, Ben Sharpe, and Tom

Steele in the finals of a tournament but with a twist. Buddy Roberts had "missed his plane" and the remaining team of Gordy and Hayes were determined to go it alone, but David Von Erich offered himself as a replacement and then won the match for the team after seventeen minutes of good action by pinning Mike Sharpe with a high knee and thus giving them the titles. Because the Von Erichs were all good-hearted Christian boys, David "did the right thing" and gave his third of the titles to Buddy Roberts on the spot, which showed a great bit of subtle acting from Michael Hayes as he quietly acted all offended that David would decline his invitation to join his little club. But it all just set up the main event when Kerry challenged Ric Flair for the World title, and Hayes slowly acted more and more evil during the match and growing frustrated with Kerry's do-gooding. Finally Hayes turned on Kerry and prevented a pin, at which point Kerry tried to leave the cage and Terry Gordy made history by slamming the door on his head, which gave Flair the tainted pin. The match actually continued for another five minutes as the first referee threw out Michael Hayes' pinfall count, but most fans remember that as the finish. Kerry lost anyway after passing out due to a concussion but, regardless, the Freebirds were instantly the biggest heels in the territory.

The company took off into the stratosphere after that and aired in markets around the country thanks to an aggressive syndication campaign from Fritz, and the Von Erich boys became gods in Texas. But fame, as usual, comes with a price, and David was the first to pay for it. The boys were treated like literal royalty in their home city and given whatever amenities they wanted in exchange for associating their names with local businesses. They were allowed to drive off the lot in brand new sports cars and motorcycles, and girls all over the state swooned at their every word. But with David dead in 1984, they needed a new star to swoon over, and though Mike Von Erich was rushed into the business long before he should have been, he was put into six-man tags with his brothers where he could at least be protected. But he fell hard and fast for the lifestyle and when a bout of toxic shock syndrome after a shoulder injury left him a total wreck, he had little left to give to the business. Despite Mike being in no condition to perform on a regular basis thanks to brain damage, he was routinely stuck on TV as "The Living Miracle," one more way for Fritz to prop up business while the Freebirds-Von Erichs feud faltered, and Mike was heart rending to watch. Reportedly Mike never wanted to be a part of the business anyway, preferring a career path that would lead into the music business, but he was born into the wrong family for that dream.

Fritz was so desperate to revive his business that he actually went out and replaced his own son with a wrestler named Kevin Vaughn. Fritz dubbed him Lance Von Erich because he happened to look a bit like the family, but the fans so completely turned on him that he was basically run out of town. But no matter how badly the fans reacted to watching their beloved promotion falling apart before their eyes, no one took it harder than Fritz, who routinely berated his poor sons for not living up to the ideals that he had worked so hard to build. After a DUI arrest of Mike triggered another meltdown from Fritz, Mike took a bottle of Placidyl out to the woods and killed himself, apologizing for everything in his suicide note but leaving his father out of any apologies given. He was only twenty-three years old when he died on April 12, 1987.

Four years later, the youngest member of the family, Chris Von Erich, chubby and totally lacking wrestling ability and charisma, debuted for the dying World Class territory (by then renamed the USWA) and was a total flop. Given the pressures to be the one to carry on the name of the family and having little chance to do so, Chris committed suicide after only a few matches into his career by shooting himself in the head with a pistol on September 12, 1991. He was only twenty-one years old. He is little more than a sad footnote in the regal family of Texas, and he could have been anything else and probably lived a full and healthy life. But Fritz wanted champion wrestlers and drove Chris to that end as surely as if he pulled the trigger himself.

But there's little argument that the biggest star of all the boys turned out to be Kerry Von Erich. He had the perfect bodybuilder's physique (straight from a steroid needle, which Fritz of course denied up and down), tons of charisma, and the high school athletics background needed to promote him as the newest star of the family. He might have even gone to the Olympics as a discus thrower, which led to his "discus punch" finisher once he became a wrestler. Kerry was basically custom-built for a career as a ready-made wrestling superstar, and that's exactly what his father expected from him and nothing less. And for the most part he lived up to those expectations. After Kerry lost to Ric Flair in the cage match on Christmas 1982, which kickstarted the legendary Freebirds v. Von Erichs feud, Fritz declared him the "uncrowned world champion" on the World Class television show, and fans in the area bought into it completely. Although David was clearly the brother who had been in line to get that title, David's death in 1984 left Kerry and Kevin as the two main members of the family. Clearly Kerry was the biggest star left, and on May 6, 1984, Fritz finally got to live out his vicarious dreams of being World champion when his son Kerry defeated Flair for the belt in a good match. It was dedicated to David's memory, complete with merchandise commemorating David that sold at ridiculous prices. It was Kerry's greatest moment, but it was also the peak of the promotion and the point when everything started going downhill. Kerry's title reign lasted only eighteen days, as Flair got it back right away once the NWA made it clear that they weren't going to risk their most important title on a guy who they were never sure was going to show up from one show to the next.

The problem was that for everything the boys were handed, they never had the maturity to deal with fame and fortune. Kerry was a noted substance abuser, and his increasing indiscretions made it tougher for Fritz to bail him out of trouble without breaking up the

squeaky clean image that the family had to project on TV. His partner in crime, Gino Hernandez, got involved in one too many drug
deals himself and ended up dead in his apartment on February 4,
1986, officially from a cocaine overdose, but many suspect murder.
Most people would learn from a friend meeting that kind of end,
but Kerry was too far gone. Fritz had already made one drug charge
disappear in 1983, when Kerry had been arrested with more than
300 assorted pills and ten grams of pot on him before the evidence
"disappeared" from the police station. Most famously, Kerry was
scheduled to do a sixty-minute draw with Ric Flair in 1984 and was
found passed out in his car minutes before the match was to begin.
His dog had died that morning and he got loaded to deal with the
grief. He was literally dragged out to the ring and Flair somehow
worked a miracle and got a watchable match out of him, but by 1986
his problems finally caught up with him.

While taking his motorcycle out and obviously intoxicated in June
1986, Kerry got into a serious wreck, crushed his ankle, and narrowly
avoided having his foot amputated. With numerous internal injuries
and what appeared to be a death wish, it seemed obvious that his
career was done. But Fritz pushed him back into the spotlight. He
got him back on TV only a month later and then back into the ring
only six months after the accident, when conventional wisdom said
that an injury like he sustained would need a year of recovery time.
It was no miracle comeback, however, because wrestling on the shattered ankle completely destroyed it, which resulted in amputation
and replacement with a prosthetic foot. This became the biggest and
most well-kept secret in wrestling, and no one found out about it
until after his death, except for one incident in 1988. He was wrestling
Colonel DeBeers at an AWA show, and during the match his boot
was accidentally pulled off and revealed nothing underneath. Fans
were shocked and the AWA immediately went into denial mode, although without pictures there was no proof and the story quickly
went away, resigned to urban legend status in the days before the

Internet. Years later Kerry could have come clean and gotten over huge as a sympathy case, but the mythology built up by his father meant that any weakness was too much.

The territory was dying despite Fritz's best efforts to save it, however, and Kerry got the World Class World heavyweight title in 1988 as a last-ditch effort to bail them out and lend them some star power. This led to an interpromotional feud against the AWA, as the two dying promotions worked together to promote *AWA SuperClash III*, which would unify the two versions of their World titles into one belt. Vince McMahon, on the WWE's DVD history of the AWA, summed it up best when he noted that the people involved in this endeavor could barely agree on ordering a cup of coffee together, let alone promoting a show. The show was a disaster and Kerry lost his belt to Jerry Lawler in a pretty good match that saw Kerry bleed buckets of blood before the match was stopped.

Despite his degenerating abilities and drug-fueled baggage, the WWF brought Kerry in for a run in 1990, replacing Brutus Beefcake as Curt Hennig's opponent at *Summerslam 90*. Kerry won the Intercontinental title from Hennig in a short bad match, and the WWF quickly realized the giant mistake they had made in taking a chance on him. He was on suicide watch and clearly needed help. After dropping the title back to Hennig (unofficial reason from the WWF: they didn't want one of their champions dropping dead on their watch) only a month later, Kerry dropped down the cards and could barely function in the ring by the end of 1991. Watching matches with him from that period of his career is embarrassing as a fan, because Kerry was completely lost in the ring and looked like he was somewhere else most of the time, even forgetting simple things during the course of the match and tripping on his own feet. By 1992, drug reform was the order of the day in the WWF locker room and anonymous tips were leading to Kerry. He was already on probation for forging prescriptions, and this shows how bad his condition was because there was no shortage of "doctors" willing to prescribe wrestlers

whatever they wanted. While on probation in January 1993 and trying to go through rehab, he was arrested again on possession charges
and now prison time was inevitable. His father couldn't save him
and he was well past the point where his star power and good looks
could carry him. On February 18, 1993, he borrowed his dad's shot-
gun and went out to the woods to "do some thinking," after giving
out his goodbyes to his few remaining loved ones. An hour later,
Fritz Von Erich went to look for him and found his body in the bush,
dead by suicide. The dream was over, and by this time neither WCW
nor the WWF even bothered to acknowledge the passing of the former Modern Day Warrior, who just a few years earlier had taken the
business by storm.

Kevin Von Erich was, and still is as of this writing, the last surviving Von Erich. Fritz's marriage fell apart in the aftermath of Chris's
death, as his wife Doris blamed him for destroying the family. Having lost his company and his entire family, he died quietly from cancer on September 10, 1997, outliving all but one of his children. I
think I should add another Bible verse to sum things up, given Fritz's
fondness for them.

> Pride goeth before destruction,
>   and an haughty spirit before a fall.
>   —Proverbs 16:18, King James version

DEATH AND WRESTLING

The death of Chris Benoit is, sadly, the furthest thing from an isolated incident. Marc Mero burned his bridges with the business by going on *Nancy Grace* following the Benoit murders, brandishing a list of dead wrestlers (numbered!) and calling for change in the industry. Although it might be a bit sensationalist to reduce his former friends to numbers (Johnny Grunge was apparently number fifteen on the list, if you're keeping score), the man had a point. Although the numbers being thrown around (anywhere from 50–100 wrestlers dying in the past ten years) may be exaggerated, there's certainly a bigger problem at play here. Clearly, people are coming into wrestling and then leaving in body bags.

Yes, I admit, Mero's list is dubious to say the least. Although the point is valid, much of the list incorporates independent wrestlers, or people who were never "stars," or people who died from what are largely natural causes. A more realistic list of top name wrestlers who dropped dead within the past ten years, and the reasons for those deaths, would read as follows.

Chris Adams

Adams died on October 7, 2001, at age 46, relatively soon after attempting to stage a comeback with WCW and doing what could be termed "not bad" with it. He has the distinction of wrestling in the first match ever to air on WCW's *Thunder* program, but his run in the big leagues didn't produce much else of note. Adams was, to say the least, a noted drug and alcohol user and abuser, which isn't terribly surprising given that he made most of his name as a top star for World Class Championship Wrestling in the '80s. Anyone partying with the Von Erichs was bound to meet a bad end, and Adams was no exception. He was probably best known for training Steve Austin in 1989 and then losing his wife to him in one of those bizarre angles gone wrong that only seem to happen in wrestling or Hollywood. And, of course, that very same thing happened again in 1996 when Kevin Sullivan lost his wife Nancy to Chris Benoit, because no one in wrestling ever learns anything despite recycling ideas over and over. Although Adams was in fact elegantly wasted at the time of his death, the death itself was not a direct result of the drugs in his system—he was "accidentally" shot by a friend during a struggle for a gun. Hearsay and rumors have since cast doubt on just how accidental this shooting was, but I'd say that either way, without the drugs and booze he'd still be alive today, rather than the wreck of a man he had turned into by the end.

Brian Adams

Died August 13, 2007, of an accidental overdose of painkillers. Not to be confused with the Canadian rock star, the death of the former Crush was a blow that hit the WWE rather harder than it might have in happier times, coming most inconveniently at a time when the promotion was trying to distance itself from the hard-partying stars of the '80s and '90s and swearing up and down that, honest, people had learned their lesson. Regardless of Adams' noninvolvement with the WWE (his last match with them was in 2001), he made his name with them and dropped dead just in time to add another statistic to a growing list while the WWE was being investigated by Congress. Adams was a guy who you always figured would get a big push based, if nothing else, on his size and spectacular hair, and for most of his career this was true. In 1990, early in his career, he was added to the reigning tag team champions, Demolition, as a replacement for Bill "Ax" Eadie. Despite being totally exposed and basically being the guy who sunk the most successful tag team of the late '80s, he was repackaged as Kona Crush and given an even bigger push as a singles wrestler and sported a mullet and day-glo tights, which apparently was supposed to make him look cool. Despite repeated attempts to make him into a top star, he never clicked with fans (mostly because he sucked so badly in the ring) and was let go after being arrested on drug possession charges. The WWF quickly played up the gun possession charges and completely ignored his steroid-related charges, but of course repackaged him and gave him yet another chance to become a star. And I'm not picking on Vince McMahon here, either, as WCW picked him up in 1998 and also spent the next two years trying to make something out of him. Ironically, his biggest success in the later stages of his career came as a tag team called Kronik with fellow stiff Bryan Clarke, as they portrayed two pot-smoking badasses. I won't even get into the whole "marijuana is or isn't a gateway drug" argument, although I've seen it act as such to a member of my immediate family and thus I'm rather more biased on the subject than some.

Mike Awesome

Died February 17, 2007. It's hard to make a case for his life being directly ended by drugs as he committed suicide by hanging, and he was generally regarded as being in a depressed state over the ending of his career and domestic troubles at the time of his death. After years of making a name for himself in Japan as a part of the Frontier Martial Arts Wrestling promotion as The Gladiator, Awesome came to prominence in 1999 with ECW. Being a smaller guy in a world of bigger wrestlers, Awesome was booked by owner Paul Heyman only in matches where his lack of size would be disguised. This strat-

egy produced a classic series of matches against the shorter Masato
Tanaka, Awesome's long-time foe in Japan. Although Heyman fooled
the fans, Awesome thought of himself as bigger than the promotion
that created him and jumped to WCW in April 2000. This move actually presented something of a tense situation for both WWF and
WCW at the time, because we hadn't seen a good old-fashioned belt-
trashing on a nationally televised wrestling show since 1995 and
everyone was a bit paranoid about seeing another one. Awesome,
you see, was the ECW champion when he left (that happened a lot
to Heyman, it seems) and WCW was deathly afraid of Awesome
showing up on Monday Nitro with the ECW World title because
everyone was pretty gun-shy about suing each other. Instead we ended
up getting Awesome dropping the title (while under contract to
WCW) to Tazz (while under contract to the WWF), who then lost the
belt to Tommy Dreamer (who was, thankfully, contracted to ECW)
in one of the strangest series of events seen in wrestling for quite a
while. And that's saying something. As for his death, he had already
announced his retirement despite a show-stealing match against
Masato Tanaka at the WWE's *One Night Stand* PPV in 2005, so technically he wasn't even an active wrestler when he died. However,
his injuries stemmed from years of drug and painkiller usage, so I'd
have to call his death at least tangentially related to drugs. I don't
think it would be a stretch to say that the years of unprotected chairs
to the head contributed to his depression, because many of the symptoms displayed by Awesome in his last days were eerily similar to
those of Benoit and other concussion cases. Certainly if he wasn't in
wrestling he'd be alive today, so that's the criteria we'll go with here.

Yokozuna

This one's pretty obviously not connected to anything he was taking, aside from ham sandwiches (if I might steal the old Mama Cass
joke). Rodney Anoia died in October 2000, weighing over 600 pounds

The Von Erich family at their peak, living up to the dream of Fritz Von Erich for at least one moment. (*Photo by wrealano@aol.com*)

Rick Rude at the top of his game with WCW, shortly before the back injury that would end his career and the drugs that would destroy his life. *(Photo by wrealano@aol.com)*

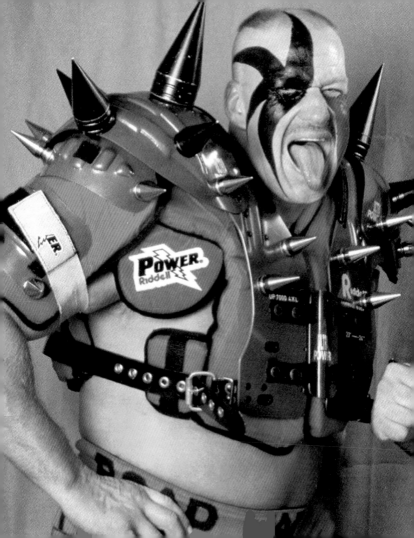

Two of the most famous wrestlers to come out of Calgary, Chris Benoit and his friend Chris Jericho, in happier days.
(Photo by wrealano@aol.com)

From the same show, Jericho demonstrates his rock star attitude years before he

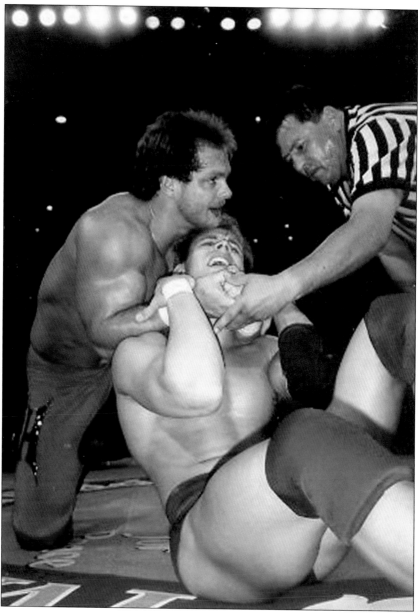

Chris Benoit chinlocks Alex Wright in WCW. Wright was another kid who was ill-prepared for everything that came along with the wrestling world and never lived up to his potential. *(Photo by wrealano@aol.com)*

Bret Hart—as he often seemed to be doing in his final days with the WWF—yelling at the fans.
(Photo by wrealano@aol.com)

The British Bulldog puts a hold on Bret Hart in the WWF.
(Photo by wrealano@aol.com)

Owen Hart is interviewed by legendary Stampede Wrestling announcer Ed Whalen. The beloved Whalen's death in 2001 tore the heart out of the Calgary wrestling community as much as anything the Hart family did.

(Photo by wrealano@aol.com)

Brian Pillman in Japan in 1991, at the peak of his high-flying powers.
(Photo by wrealano@aol.com)

Bad News Allen Coage, who reputedly made Andre the Giant stand down in an altercation early in his career. He also died, but thankfully from natural causes.
(Photo by wrealano@aol.com)

Sylvester "Junkyard Dog" Ritter, who could have been as big as Hulk Hogan
but chose to wreck his life with cocaine instead.

(Photo by wrealano@aol.com)

Louis Spicoli holds an abdominal stretch on Chris Benoit in 1995.
(Photo by wrealano@aol.com)

A very sad shot of three doomed wrestlers in happier times.
(Photo by wrealano@aol.com)

The lovely Elizabeth, just a few days before her death.
(Photo by wrealano@aol.com)

Chris Benoit, about to execute a victory roll on current WWE announcer Tazz.
(Photo by wrealano@aol.com)

Just like wrestling, Hollywood also has a history of living fast and dying young, as Bret Hart seems to ponder here. *(Photo by wrealano@aol.com)*

and no longer able to work for the WWF because he couldn't get medical clearance to do so in twenty states. Although wrestling is known for rewarding size, his size was a different type and he was more of a freakshow act than a serious worker.

Rodney debuted in 1985 after being trained by his Samoan relatives Afa & Sika, and though still a teenager he was already pushing 400 pounds. Dubbed The Great Kokina, he became something of a big attraction in Mexico and later Japan, where he teamed with Vader. This earned him a shot in the AWA for a brief time as Kokina Maximus and, with that kind of national exposure and a freakshow appeal, it was only a matter of time before the WWF came calling. Vince wanted a sumo wrestling monster, someone who could be gigantic without the need for steroids, but it's perhaps ironic that even though he was pressured to get bigger by natural means (i.e., eating) that was almost as deadly to him as the drugs might have been. Trying to emulate the sumo look, he shot from 400 pounds to 500 pounds and was rewarded with an equally gigantic push in the fall of 1992. The message has always been clear: Wrestling promoters care more about the gimmick than the person, and will pressure wrestlers to do whatever they have to in order to meet that image. No one was even able to knock him off his feet, and he steamrolled through the 1993 Royal Rumble to earn a shot at Bret Hart and the WWF World title at Wrestlemania IX.

This of course was a disaster of epic proportions, but Rodney won the title in a short bad match and then dropped it to Hulk Hogan literally a minute after winning it, thus losing his first title defense and looking like a joke in the process. Hogan's fifth World title reign was supposed to re-energize the company and allow him to "pass the torch" to Bret Hart, but Hogan balked at dropping the title to someone as small as Bret, and thus Yokozuna got it back at the first *King of the Ring* PPV. Yoko did pretty good business as a monster heel champion, but Vince had something bigger in mind: creating the next Hulk Hogan. So Lex Luger, the most undeserving guy you could imagine, slammed Yokozuna aboard the USS *Intrepid* and got pushed to the moon. And I mean it was almost literal, because if they could have put him on the space shuttle and had him do a publicity shoot on the moon, they would have. It was in fact the largest promotional push ever given to a wrestler, including Hulk Hogan, and after touring the country in a bus the natural payoff would have been Luger winning the WWF title from evil foreign menace Yokozuna. Instead, they decided to prolong the chase to *Wrestlemania X* and gave him a countout win instead, but that only added to his existing reputation as a choker and pretty much killed his momentum. Luger never got that title. Yokozuna's next brush with major embarrassment came at *Royal Rumble 94*, as he successfully defended the WWF title against Undertaker by having ten guys stuff him into a coffin. And Undertaker "rose to the heavens" after a soliloquy, supposedly dead and buried. It was definitely a rough time to be a wrestling fan, let me tell you.

After dropping the belt back to Bret Hart at *Wrestlemania X*, instead of Luger as was original planned months before, Yoko's weight got even more out of control as he fell down the card. He returned the next year, at the disappointing *Wrestlemania XI* as Owen Hart's surprise tag team partner, and they won the WWF tag titles from the Smoking Gunns. Despite supposed ultimatums from the WWF to slim down for his own health, Yokozuna returned bigger than ever and got almost as big of a push. This would be echoed again with Big Show years later as his weight problems spiraled out of control for much of his tenure in the company, and yet he continued to be employed and win titles no matter how fat he got. This would prove to be Yoko's last major run in the sport, because they dropped the belts back to the Gunns six months later and Yoko was never a major factor again. His weight ballooned as he refused to attend weight-loss programs, and he was not only becoming an embarrassment to the company because of his mobility programs, but a liability due to his size. His contract was not renewed and he made his final appearance with the WWF at *Survivor Series 96*. WCW made overtures to bring him in on more than one occasion, but the deal always fell through. His last appearance of note in wrestling was at the momentously stupid *Heroes of Wrestling* PPV in October 1999, teaming with Jake Roberts in a match where Roberts showed up too drunk to actually compete and fondled his snake (the real one, not the metaphoric one) on live TV.

Would he be alive today if not for wrestling? Doubtful. At his worst, post-WWE, he was 800 pounds and a walking tombstone. Although you can blame Vince for pressuring him to increase his size in 1992, Vince also realized the error of his ways and put even more pressure on him to lose weight afterward, wanting him at 400 pounds to continue his employment. That being said, he was a name and the WWF kept giving him chance after chance until they were medically prohibited from doing so. He might not have died of drugs (although he was a heavy user of painkillers late in his career), but death was inevitable in this case and you have to put most of the blame on his WWF career, in my opinion.

Bam Bam Bigelow

Scott "Bam Bam" Bigelow, who died in January 2007, was always an interesting guy, but here's a case where wrestling destroyed his life, no question. Certainly when you're naturally 300 pounds and taking bumps like he did, you're going to have to rely on painkillers to get through. Indeed, Bigelow was a long-time user of Oxycontin, one of the most potent ones. Although Bigelow achieved arguably his greatest degree of fame in 1995 with a main event slot at *Wrestlemania XI*, he fell on hard times after that. His WCW career was a bust, consisting mainly of Hardcore title matches and playing third banana to DDP and Kanyon. Following WCW's closing in 2001, Bigelow sat out his contract with Time-Warner, but he suffered second-degree burns over forty percent of his body while rescuing kids from a fire.

In 2005, he nearly killed girlfriend Janis Remiesiewicz in a car accident that police would have treated as a homicide investigation had she died. In fact this was almost a relief to Bigelow's friends, because he had essentially vanished off the face of the earth a few years before and no one knew of his whereabouts. His actual death was caused by a lethal combination of cocaine and benzodiazepine (an anti-anxiety drug), which showed the kind of state of mind he was in at the time. Coupled with an already problematic heart and diabetes, it was a recipe for death. Clearly this was someone who had a long-time problem and wasn't going to receive help for it from either major promotion that he worked for.

Biff Wellington

Shayne Bower died in June 2007, which was perhaps one of the many things that led to Chris Benoit going off the deep end a few days later. Certainly they were good friends and his death might have hit Benoit hard, but we'll never know. Wellington, who was long past his wrestling prime at the time of his death, died of a heart attack, likely caused by a drug overdose, in his parents' house. He was an admitted user of painkillers and had several notable injuries that left him out of action for long periods of time, which probably didn't help to alleviate his painkiller problems. A family friend noted in an interview with Slam! Wrestling that "I know it wasn't drugs, because I know Shayne. He'd had a real battle with drugs, and he'd been clean for the last two years." It's definitely another case where life on the road directly led to his death, although he never worked for either of the Big Two on a regular basis so it's not like you can blame them.

Chris Candido

Died April 28, 2005. If ever there was a tragedy waiting to happen, it's Candido. His drug and alcohol problems were extremely public thanks to a rather sleazy attempt by ECW owner Paul Heyman to get Tammy Sytch back into the spotlight in 1999. Admittedly the problems were more publicly Tammy's than Chris's, but he was always in her shadow anyway. Candido himself was always something of an indy darling, more admired by other wrestlers than fans, and the furthest he ever got on the national stage was as half of the WWF tag team champions with Tom Pritchard.

Despite some very low points in his career (like working independent dates with a very bloated Tammy while fighting through rehab and legal troubles), Candido was making a comeback with TNA in 2005 and was apparently clean and sober. It's the weird nature of the wrestling business where a thirty-three-year-old wrestler was acting as the veteran adviser to a younger team, but that was his role and he worked it quite well. An ankle injury during a six-man match seemingly ended his comeback attempt, but things got worse when he went in for surgery and was pronounced dead two days later.

Stories on the cause of death differ: Official word was that the ankle became infected (a possible side-effect of any surgery) and he died in his weakened state, ironically refusing drugs to help combat it due to his ongoing recovery from addiction. Tammy Sytch tells a different story that blames the doctors for not warning him about the dangers of flying after surgery and listing the cause of death as a blood clot that formed and travelled to his heart due to flying.

The results of the autopsy were never made public, but either way it's apparent that drugs, a demon he battled his whole career, were not a direct factor in his death. Small consolation, I suppose. That being said, his death came directly as a result of an injury sustained in the ring, which opens up another can of worms entirely about safe working conditions. Would he be alive today if not for wrestling? Hard to guess, actually. Tammy was equally involved in the drug life, and she's still alive and trying for another WWE job, so anything is possible.* Things weren't looking good for Chris for a long time, however, and I'd tend to think that had a freak accident not ended his life, something far worse might have.

Bobby Duncum Jr.

Died January 24, 2000. Aha, so now we come to the first person on our list to actually die while under contract to one of the Big Two, in this case WCW. Although the WWE seems to enjoy putting the blame for drug-related deaths squarely at the feet of The Other Guy in their press releases, it was something of a rarity for WCW talent to actually die while under contract. Say what you will about Eric Bischoff's cut-throat business mentality when it came to talent, but he knew when to cut bait on someone before they went and died. Duncum never really had a distinguished career, and mostly acted as the tag team partner for bigger acts like a young John Bradshaw Leyfield or Stan Hansen, but his story is a familiar one: Found dead at a young age due to accidental overdose from prescription painkillers. Clearly a direct case of someone getting injured and falling back on drugs to medicate themselves, and I'm 100 percent certain he'd still be alive if not for wrestling. Furthermore, his father was a fairly big star, and it's the familiar story of the son trying to live up to the famous name of his dad, which we've seen all too often in wrestling as well.

Anthony "Pitbull #2" Durante

Died September 26, 2003. Now here's a guy who was destined to wind up dead. Not only was he obviously a heavy steroid user—he looked like a walking He-Man action figure—but later in his career

---

*In addition to admitting that she used drugs in an interview on ECW's TV program in 1999, Tammy Sytch has been quite upfront about her previous addictions in her other interviews since then and on her website.

he and partner Gary Wolfe started diversifying by *selling* drugs as well as taking them.* And when the government indicted him for doing so, he turned state's evidence against other dealers and more or less put a bullseye on his own head. For kicks, he and his wife made homemade Oxycontin (a word I seem to be typing a lot during this overview) and, say it with me, accidentally overdosed on painkillers. The Pitbulls achieved only a marginal level of fame in their careers, so maybe Durante felt that dealing drugs was a good career to fall back on, I dunno. His partner, Gary Wolfe, actually suffered a broken neck in 1997 and I can almost understand him getting hooked on painkillers as a result, but Durante just came across as a rotten human being who was going to end up dead one way or the other. It's hard to blame this one on anyone but himself.

The Public Enemy (Johnny Grunge and Rocco Rock)

Died February 16, 2006 and September 21, 2002, respectively. Ted "Rocco Rock" Petty was by far the more accomplished worker of the duo. He started as a high flying star named The Cheetah Kid and moved on through a series of nothing gimmicks (like a one-shot deal with WCW as "Colonel DeClerk" for their "international" tag team tournament in 1990) before Paul Heyman saw him working on an independent show in 1993 and decided that he'd make a great tag team partner for another guy he was grooming for stardom.

Mike "Johnny Grunge" Durham was a good friend of Chris Benoit and probably one of the reasons why Benoit was so depressed about friends dropping dead. Although Durham's death, at age thirty-nine and while weighing over 400 pounds, was glossed over at the time as just one of those things, the proverbial shit hit the fan after Benoit's

---

*Gary Wolfe was put on three years' probation in New York in 1998 for selling drugs—this is a matter of public record.

death. With celebrity doctor Phil Astin under the microscope, it was discovered that he had essentially been prescribing Durham pills like they were candy, specifically the dangerous muscle relaxer known as Soma. Astin had prescribed 120 of them to Durham the day before his death and as Dr. William Monroe explained on *Nancy Grace* during the Benoit fallout:

> Those are two bad words to say together. Hydrocodone is commonly called Vicodin, and it`s mixed with Tylenol. It is a schedule three substance. Soma is a really good drug. I only use it in the hospital, though. I never give it in the office because of its addictive potential. Soma`s metabolites are also addictive. The number one side effect from an overdose of Hydrocodone would be respiratory depression. The number one side effect of Soma at higher doses would be respiratory depression. And you put those two together, and that spells trouble.

Trouble, indeed, as Durham's official cause of death was complications from sleep apnea caused by his weight and an existing heart condition, and the drugs alone were not enough to kill him. The source of the heart condition? Years of taking steroids, of course! Now keep in mind, Durham wasn't exactly a cruiserweight or a bodybuilder in his leanest years, so this begs the question as to why someone who wrestled with his shirt on would want to bother with steroids in the first place, or indeed do them in the kind of amounts that were prescribed to him by Dr. Astin. Durham's widow, Penny, explains his reasoning, again from *Nancy Grace*:

> That`s what they all did. And not only that, he said it made him feel invincible when he got out in the ring, that he felt like he could take the world on, and you know, jump off the

ladders, jump through tables, and to do all the things that they did in the ring.

To me, that statement is the biggest indictment of the system. Wrestlers have long had a "if you jump off a bridge then I have to also" mentality (sometimes literally . . .), and steroids have been so ingrained in the system that people who would not normally get involved with them end up drugged to the gills because that's what they feel is expected of them. Even more frightening are the rages that come from using the amounts that Durham was into. Again, Penny's words:

> Yes, one time, we were—you know, we were just having a conversation and talking, and you know, just—and drank a couple beers, and he just went off, and he came after me with the butcher knife. And I got down on my knees and I just started praying—and I just started praying, and then it just started dissipating.

According to Penny, her husband got pills in such volume that local pharmacies refused to fill them any longer. Durham, who was deteriorating rapidly, gained weight with an already large frame and struggled to find work. After earning up to $300,000 a year in his prime with WCW, he was reduced to looking for work with his father-in-law's carpet installation business. Even then, however, he took huge amounts of painkillers every day and couldn't function like a normal human being, and often passed out while doing simple tasks like driving the company van.

By the time he died in February 2006, he was separated from his wife and living in the trailer of friend Eric Zinck, who would do runs to the pharmacy to pick up Durham's prescriptions when his friend was too medicated to get out of bed. Clearly this is a case where wrestling was a direct cause of his death, and actually drove him to the behavior he exhibited, which turned into a vicious circle of steroids to increase the risks in the ring and then painkillers to deal with the injuries caused by those risks.

By contrast, Petty was almost a choirboy compared to his partner, who was not known for being a drug user of any magnitude. At the same time, he also died of a heart attack, and we've seen that the common cause is generally painkillers and steroids, so perhaps he wasn't as innocent as he seemed.

Hercules Hernandez

Died March 6, 2004, another victim of a heart attack. I don't know if an autopsy was ever released to the public, but he was a heavy user of steroids and it likely led to the heart disease that ended his life. Hercules was definitely part of the "old school" mentality of partying in the 1980s. His death wasn't particularly notable and he didn't achieve much more than midcard status at his peak.

Terry "Bamm Bamm" Gordy

Died July 16, 2001, from a heart attack. This case is a complete and total slam dunk on the side of the party lifestyle leading directly to the death of a wrestler, as Gordy was one of the most promising and talented workers to come out of the South, before a drug overdose at age thirty-two put him into a coma and essentially fried his brain. The Gordy that emerged and continued working long past when he should have given it up was a shell of his former self as he lumbered around the ring and looked lost most of the time.

Gordy actually debuted at age thirteen after dropping out of school in the ninth grade, and you have to wonder about the unscrupulous promoter who agreed to give him that gig. He progressed up the card quickly, and worked in territories like the Poffos' ICW

as "Terry Mecca" and then moved to Memphis, where he hooked up
as the tag team partner of another teenaged hellraiser named Michael
Seitz, aka Michael Hayes. They were an instant hit, as Gordy was
rapidly improving as a worker and Hayes was the mouthpiece to
carry the team and generate the buzz. Hayes credits his idea for using
"Freebird" as their entrance music and the rock concert-like atmosphere of their entrance to years of working at southern concerts and
seeing the audience crossover. Initially promoters thought he was
high (which he probably was), but the concept caught fire and the
Fabulous Freebirds were born. By 1979, they were too big for the territory and egos were threatened, so they left for Bill Watts' Mid-South
and added Buddy Roberts, himself already a veteran degenerate who
fit right in with the drinking and partying of the Freebirds.

The Freebirds, besides being credited as one of the first groups
to use rock music in their act, was also the innovator of a conceit
unique to professional wrestling: Three people holding the tag team
titles. Although I suppose it's akin to baseball teams being able to
change their lineup from night to night, it's always struck me as
weird that wrestling would feature two people winning a title and
then a third person being allowed to defend it. Certainly the idea of
three-man teams was not unknown in Mexican wrestling, but even
there, it was generally an actual three-man tag team title to compete
for. When they won the National tag team titles in 1980, they became the first tag team I know of to use that gimmick, although they
influenced many other teams in the future. The Russians (Ivan &
Nikita Koloff and Barry "Krusher Khruschev" Darsow) used a similar trick when they won the NWA World tag titles in 1985. Demolition was the next team to recycle the trick, as Bill "Ax" Eadie and
Barry Darsow (this time as Smash) subbed in Brian "Crush" Adams
in 1990 to reduce the workload on Eadie. In fact, it was the teaming
of Smash and Crush who lost the titles. In 1998, the same trick was
done with a twist in WCW, as Raven won the WCW World tag titles with partners Perry Saturn and Chris Kanyon, only to see Kanyon

turn on him and switch allegiances to the "Jersey Triad" of Dallas
Page and Bam Bam Bigelow, thus employing the same two-out-of-
three gimmick.

Gordy and the Freebirds were a huge success for Bill Watts, and
drew huge numbers on top, including one of the most famous angles of all time: blinding Junkyard Dog with their deadly "Freebird
Cream," which resulted in Dog supposedly being blind during the
birth of his daughter and returning for revenge in front of 30,000
fans at the New Orleans Superdome. What really sold the angle was
Dog's dedication to it outside of the ring, as he made sure to always
wear dark glasses around the city and carried on the act with anyone who wasn't inside the business already. Part of the cool factor
for the Freebirds was their interviews, where they'd glorify the drug-
induced experiences on the so-called "Badstreet USA," and Gordy
himself was well known for his fondness for Jack Daniels whiskey.
These days you probably wouldn't hear someone going on a supposedly family-friendly program and bragging about getting stoned
(unless you're Rob Van Dam, I guess) because it would be a pretty
big warning sign, but it was different then.

But even with the success the Freebirds achieved for Watts, it
was nothing compared to what they did in World Class in 1983,
which essentially changed wrestling forever. The Freebirds vs. Von
Erichs feud that dominated from 1983–1987 was violent and intense
and redefined what a wrestling television show was all about, and
Gordy was one of the biggest reasons why it worked so well. Gordy
was now an international star and the show was an instant hit, and
Fritz Von Erich made history by syndicating the show all over the
world, years before Vince McMahon would do the same thing with
the WWF. With the Von Erichs representing the Christian viewpoint
and the Freebirds living the rock 'n' roll, drug-fueled lifestyle, the
show was a natural morality play and a perfect fit for strange out-
lets like the Christian Broadcasting Network, where it was a huge
hit. Ironically, although the Freebirds portrayed the hard-living, hard-

drinking debauchers, it was the Von Erich boys who were truly living that life, and who paid the ultimate price for it. More importantly to the history of the wrestling, Michael Hayes introduced World Class producer/director Keith Mitchell to the idea of doing vignettes in between matches to build up characters for the wrestlers on the show, an idea that would mysteriously become Vince McMahon's "innovation" when Mitchell was snapped up by the WWF years later. It was a change that turned wrestling from the typical image of sweaty guys in tights into the male-oriented soap opera that most people know it as today.

Once the World Class territory inevitably cooled down again, Gordy moved on to Japan, where he was an immediate sensation. He brought the powerbomb with him, the first person to do it in the days before it became the finisher of choice for every crappy worker over 300 pounds in the business, and soon Gordy gained a reputation as one of the best workers in the world. He brought the experience from the Japanese style back to the U.S. and was given the first UWF World title in 1986. Gordy returned to work for Bill Watts as he attempted to take the former Mid-South territory onto the national stage. It would prove to be his peak as a singles wrestler in the U.S., unfortunately. Gordy returned to Texas after the UWF fell apart and found himself involved in an angle that was pretty skeevy even by wrestling standards, as he and Roberts attacked aging Fritz Von Erich and caused him to have a "heart attack." Fans were given updates on Fritz's condition from the hospital, which would vary up and down depending on how well the shows were doing that week. Considering the morbid ends for Fritz's family even at that point, this angle was pretty much over the line, and Gordy departed for Japan again.

Although Gordy had been breaking down and suffering from knee problems even at a relatively young age, he was teamed up with Steve Williams and they became the Miracle Violence Connection. In addition to having one of the best tag team names I've ever heard, they dominated All Japan for three years and were quite bad-ass to boot. An overdose by Gordy in 1990 should have been a wakeup call for everyone, but instead only resulted in a minor de-push and the steamroll continued for Gordy and Williams. They set ratings records in Japan and were so hot that Bill Watts brought them into WCW in 1992 once he took it over, and they won both the WCW and newly recreated NWA World tag titles in the span of two weeks. Their Japan commitments meant that they enjoyed only a short reign, but it only added to their legend in Japan, and Gordy was making the biggest money of his life despite only being half of a tag team. And then it all ended.

In August 1993, Gordy was on a plane back to Japan and in pain again, so he took fifty Somas, which is actually a number not out of line with what a lot of wrestlers take to endure injuries suffered in the ring. Think about that the next time you take two Advil for a headache. Gordy turned blue and EMTs had to revive him after his heart stopped beating, and he ended up in a coma for five days and suffered brain damage as a result. He could no longer talk or walk, let alone wrestle, but even this wasn't enough of a hint for him. He was a kid who had dropped out of school and didn't know anything else, and without any money saved he had to continue wrestling to pay bills.

Subsequent attempts by Gordy to return to the ring were more sad than anything. He ended with a pathetic run in the WWF as The Executioner, the second banana to Mankind who acted as a whipping boy for the Undertaker before he disappeared from the wrestling world for good. I don't think anyone can argue that Gordy didn't throw his career away, but this one almost falls under that nebulous "personal choice" category that Ken Kennedy likes to talk about. Certainly anyone who watched Gordy wrestle would never argue that he was a steroid user, and his drug use likely came from being a dumb kid as much as anything. It's just another lesson that wrestling can seduce and destroy even the most talented and give nothing

back, as everyone knew about Gordy's habits and no one did anything to help him until it was too late.

Eddie Guerrero

Died November 13, 2005, of congenital heart failure worsened by
years of steroids and growth hormone abuse. I covered most of his
WWE career in my last book, but I'm always happy to share thoughts
on Eddie. Despite his great matches on WCW TV, I always got the
sense that he was too small to be used in the role that he was being
shoehorned into and that can be bothersome. It's one thing to suddenly push somebody to a higher level, but if you haven't established them at that level yet, it's ultimately meaningless. Such was
the case with Eddie's WCW U.S. title tournament victory over Diamond Dallas Page in 1996, a guy who really should have been getting the title himself at that point. Eddie was given the win although
he wasn't established as anything more than a mid-level babyface in
the company with no personality and no reason for the fans to care
about the title win. Keep in mind that his peak with WCW didn't
come until two years after this win, and only after he had firmly established himself on the dark side of things. It really showed the first
lesson that Eddie's career taught: You can't just stick someone smaller
into the heavyweight division and expect people to buy it. You have
to build them up as a heavyweight and give people a reason to care.
A heel turn in 1997, which brought Eddie's "rudo" personality from
Mexico to the forefront in WCW, made him into the star of the cruiser-
weight division and a Match of the Year candidate against Rey Mysterio Jr., at Halloween Havoc that year seemed to be the combination
needed to really shoot him into the ranks of the main event stars.
But it didn't.

In fact, Guerrero's frustrations with the political scene backstage
were well publicized and best summed up by an incident in 1998
when a heated discussion over money with Eric Bischoff turned into

Eddie getting hit with a cup of coffee. Eddie denied that it was actually intentional on Bischoff's part, but you just can't make stuff like that up. However, Eddie's frustrations with WCW evolved from more sinister effects than just flying cups of coffee, as the constant travel and life away from home were increasingly driving him to drugs and alcohol, common problems for wrestlers on the road to be sure. Doubly so for an addictive personality like Eddie's, and having a famous name to live up to just added to the pressure. By 1999, his stalled push and drug problems led to him falling asleep at the wheel and hitting a telephone pole at 130 MPH, which seemingly resulted in his exit from the sport. However, Eddie's stubborn nature asserted itself, and he was back in six weeks from what should have been a career-ending accident, but in this case not for the better. Returning too early led him to fall even further into painkillers and booze to kill the (literal) pain, and he celebrated this newfound hobby by overdosing and nearly dying. Say what you will about the WWE, but they never let stuff like that slide and Eddie would have been sent to rehab or fired immediately. WCW, however, was not that kind of organization, and Eddie's problems were swept under the rug until his departure in 2000, along with the other "Radicalz," which signaled the beginning of the end of WCW.

Eddie's bad luck continued immediately upon entering the WWE, as a match with the New Age Outlaws on Smackdown resulted in him breaking his arm in his debut, which was kind of appropriate given his life's direction. However, when he returned, it was with something he had never really been given in WCW—a character to play. Carrying out a decidedly silly storyline with unlikely romantic partner Chyna, Eddie's personality was allowed to shine through even as Jerry Lawler shrieked "Latino Heat!" in irritating fashion on a regular basis to get the character over. It was insulting and racist in some ways, but Eddie made it work. For anyone else, that probably would have been the thing to kill their career, but Eddie was the guy with the charisma to pull it off.

Unfortunately, the whole time that he was developing that character, he was also hiding an addiction to painkillers, which only his closest friends knew about. Despite his carefree character on-screen, his real life was becoming such a mess that Chris Benoit went to the office and stooged Eddie out to Jim Ross for his own good. Given a choice between rehab or firing, he chose rehab. It didn't stick, and Eddie hit rock bottom in 2001 with a drunk driving arrest, and this time he wasn't given a choice. The WWE fired him to send a message to the other employees (Brian "Grandmaster Sexay" Lawler was similarly fired for drug-related problems around the same time) and this seemed to be the end of the Eddie Guerrero story.

However, Eddie was nothing if not doggedly stubborn, and he was unwilling to accept anything but a return to the big stage. He went through rehab, despite the loss of his marriage, cleaned himself up, and began working independent dates to show the WWE that he could be depended on to stay sober without supervision. In fact, he was never to fall into addiction again, which showed that you really do need to be allowed to hit rock bottom on your own before you can get better. When Eddie returned in 2002, it was a leaner, meaner Eddie Guerrero who immediately captured the Intercontinental title from Rob Van Dam and put on fantastic matches with him. A move to Smackdown and the U.S. title came next, and he teamed with nephew Chavo and carried the tag team division. And then something extraordinary happened.

As a "hook" for the Guerrero tag team, they had filmed silly vignettes featuring the Guerreros lying, cheating, and stealing from unsuspecting victims in order to put over what kind of bad people they really were. However, what it told the audience was that they were smarter than everyone else, and wrestling fans will always cheer the smarter person. And when Chavo was injured at the beginning of 2003 and Eddie won the tag titles with temporary partner Tajiri, fans clearly regarded Eddie as the star of the team. A supposed heel turn by Eddie in fact became a face turn, as fans sided with Eddie's outrage over Tajiri scratching his low-rider. I mean, who wouldn't? More than that, once Eddie won the U.S. title, he began booking his own finishes, and came up with increasingly unique and brilliant ways to retain the belt through trickery. His favorite bit of deception was to use the title belt as a weapon, then feign unconsciousness and put the belt in the hands of his opponent to make himself look like the victim. Although this maneuver was supposed to make him a bad person, it made his opponents look stupid instead, and thus Eddie became a star again, two years after he had been written off by the business. More importantly, ratings with Hispanic communities were through the roof for his segments, and he was one of the few people to draw real money at the time. By November 2003, the writing was on the wall, and they could no longer delay a very real push for him. Eddie won the WWE World title from Brock Lesnar at No Way Out 2004 in front of a sympathetic crowd and successfully defended against Kurt Angle at Wrestlemania XX, where he celebrated with Chris Benoit. Sadly, this marked the last real high point of his life.

The pressures of being champion and temptations to go back to his former habits got the best of him just a few months after winning the title, and the belt was put on John Bradshaw Leyfield for Eddie's own good in July 2004, but left him much happier in the midcard. Another heel turn and an extended feud with tag partner Rey Mysterio seemed to have jumpstarted his career and he was ready to win his second World title, this one from Batista in November 2005, but just a few hours before the scheduled title change he was found dead of a heart attack in his hotel room, as years of steroid usage and drugs combined with a congenital heart problem to get the best of him.

Obviously, Eddie's death should have been the catalyst for sweeping changes in the system long before Chris Benoit forced the issue. Eddie was a young wrestler, in the prime of his career, and ready to reclaim the World title, and he had just come off an inspirational autobiography and DVD about how he was clean and sober. This was shocking to many people who didn't understand that there's "clean" and then there's really clean. His death did have a few immediate impacts, like the Wellness Program that we'll get more into later, but besides a tribute show I don't think that the message that should have been imparted by his passing ever quite made it through. Eddie was part of the generation that was supposed to be "different," the generation that was supposed to have learned from the stupid mistakes of the '80s and given up the life of excess in favor of videogames and MySpace like the current one has supposedly done. And yet as his death showed, even if you defeat your demons, they can still come back and defeat you. I think Eddie is almost a sadder case than Benoit because everyone thought that he had figured out his problem and dealt with it, and in the end he still died because of it.

Eddie's death was ruled a heart attack due to the long-term effects of steroid usage and painkillers, not to mention the heart being enlarged by years of using human growth hormone. And yet even though I have to continue typing "heart attack brought on by years of drug use," people still don't see the correlation between wrestling and the deaths that infest it. Eddie's death was one that hurt me on a personal level, not only because I was such a huge fan of his, but because the WWE not only didn't take any meaningful steps to prevent other deaths following his, but they actually attempted to cash in on it.

Russ Haas

Died December 15, 2001, of a heart attack. Not really on the list for any reason other than he is one of the few and proud to die while under WWE contract, or more specifically a developmental contract in OVW. He was successful on the indy circuit as a tag team with his brother, and current WWE star, Charlie Haas, but he suffered a heart attack and was prohibited from wrestling again. But he did anyway, suffered a second one, and died. Can't say they didn't warn him here.

Road Warrior Hawk

Died October 19, 2003 of a heart attack. This is another death that people can't say they didn't see coming. It's also one where the problem wasn't so much ignored as shamelessly mocked on national TV by people who should have known better. This case is also another running theme of this book: where a wrestler finds Jesus, repents all his sins, and then dies anyway because even religion can't cure a heart damaged by years of steroid abuse. For every Ted Dibiase and Nikita Koloff who can go that route and clean up their life, there's a Hawk.

Years before the Road Warriors became the biggest and most influential tag team in the history of, well, everything, Mike Hegstrand was working as a bouncer in a club in Minneapolis. He was part of a graduating class of 1976 that included future wrestling stars Curt Hennig, Rick Rude, Brady Boone, and Tom Zenk. Of course, only Zenk remains alive as of this writing. By the time you read this, who knows? On the WWE's DVD of their life, Animal shared a story about how they'd have contests to see who could toss bums out the farthest, and then would go watch wrestling and talk about how the wrestlers were all wimps who wouldn't stand a chance against them. After a meeting with future star and Governor Jesse Ventura, they were told they would never stand a chance in the business but were given the number of famous trainer Eddie Sharkey anyway. Wrestling training, according to Animal, was tougher than they thought it would be, which is quite possibly a candidate for the most obvious statement ever uttered on a WWE DVD release, but Sharkey was impressed with their size if nothing else. And I mean *nothing* else, because both Hegstrand (working in Canada initially as a German named

Crusher Von Haig) and future partner Joe "Animal" Laurinaitis were truly awful out of the gate.

However, in a plot twist right out of the Vince McMahon play-book years later, Georgia Championship Wrestling booker Ole Anderson saw the movie *The Road Warrior* with Mel Gibson and decided he wanted a leather-clad biker bad-ass for his promotion. Laurinaitis got the job but was so horrible he was returned to wrestling school within a week. However, Ole's cheap nature was on the side of the future tag team. In Ole's eyes, the promotion had been losing money because of excessive spending on frivolous expenses like big name stars, and his plan was to develop his own stars using no-name guys who looked like stars. So Hegstrand and Laurinaitis were picked at random, given the Road Warriors name that Ole liked so much, and put with Paul Ellering as a manager. They even managed to "win" a tournament for the tag team titles before they even stepped foot in the territory, something that only wrestlers can ever accomplish. But that didn't matter because—in one of the few times you can say that someone revolutionized the business without having it sound like hyperbole—they took the promotion by storm. Fans and opponents had no idea what to make of these two giant musclemen, who threw jobbers around the ring like ragdolls and never backed down or took punishment, but one thing everyone knew: They were *stars*.

Ellering also managed King Kong Bundy and Jake Roberts, and together the stable was known as The Legion of Doom, although over time Roberts and Bundy left the group and the Road Warriors basically inherited that moniker in addition to their own team name. Either one was fitting, certainly. Although Ole Anderson was the guy who brought them in and had them squash jobbers in record time in order to hide their, shall we say, technical deficiencies, it was Bill Watts who added his two cents and gave them the spiked leather and facepaint to really hammer home the psychological warfare that made them famous.

But as was generally inevitable with Ole Anderson running things,

Georgia Championship Wrestling was dying a slow death, and in 1984
Vince McMahon bought their time slot on TBS and the Road Warriors
decided to seek greener pastures. So it was back home to Minnesota,
as Hulk Hogan's surging popularity was increasing business for Verne
Gagne and the AWA, and the Warriors were a good fit there. At the
same time, Verne had no idea what to do with them besides putting
the tag belts on them and hoping for the best, and bruised egos abounded.
Although they were certainly selling more in the AWA than they had
in their initial Georgia run, there was no one to challenge them physically at that point. As a result, in fans' eyes, supposedly legendary
teams like the High Flyers were completely exposed as jokes when
put next to the massive Warriors. The Road Warriors were supposed
to be heels, but they were booked so dominantly that fans cheered
them because everyone else was weak and impotent next to them.
It finally took Larry Hennig beating the crap out of Hawk one night,
when Hawk's selling was particularly stingy, for the Warriors to
loosen up and give opponents anything at all in the ring. Finally,
after a feud with the Fabulous Ones (Stan Lane and Steve Keirn) was
so ridiculously one-sided that it turned the Warriors babyface by default and drove the Fabs out of the promotion, Verne made the turn
official and brought in the Fabulous Freebirds to draw something
with the Warriors. That didn't work either, and the Warriors started
touring Japan and NWA member territories and drew crazy money
everywhere they went. Except with Verne. Funny how that worked.

They finally dropped the AWA tag titles to the oddball pairing
of Jimmy Garvin and Steve Regal (not Darrin Matthews, aka William
Regal in WWE and Stephen Regal in WCW) and departed for Jim
Crockett Promotions permanently, where a feud with the Russians
was the order of the day. Ironically, two of the Russians (Scott "Nikita
Koloff" Simpson and Barry "Khrusher Khruschev" Darsow) were in
fact from Minnesota, like the Road Warriors. The third one, Ivan Koloff,
was from Canada. But that's wrestling for you. Regardless, the fans
were rabid to see the superpowerful teams clash, and where there's

a hot feud, there's Dusty Rhodes. He instantly became the Warriors' best friend and six-man tag partner, and even won the newly created World Six-Man titles with them. By this time, the team had really gotten into a groove with a distinctive interview style that distinguished them from other muscle-head teams on the circuit. Animal would hit whatever points needed to be hit for any current feud they were in, pass it off to Hawk with "Tell 'em, Hawk!", and then Hawk would wrap it up with a totally unrelated threat of bodily harm. Some of my favorites included "When we're done with you, your face is gonna look like it was on fire and they tried to put it out with an axe" and "When we're done with you boys, we're going for relatives!" Poor Paul Ellering was always left to summarize their ramblings and bring them back on point, but then that's what they paid him for.

The Warriors were so hot by 1986 that they attempted to push Hawk as a single for much of the year in matches with Ric Flair that suffered from the same screwjob finish that was killing the company—the Dusty finish. It went like this: Referee got knocked out, Hawk tossed Flair over the top rope and then scored the pin off something else, second referee counted the pin and awarded him the title, first referee revived and reversed the decision, repeated until the territory is dead. They killed more cities than can be counted on two hands with that finish, as disgusted fans stopped coming back to see the rematch. Hawk's pinnacle as a single came when he headlined the Great American Bash tour against Flair, but with the same finish in Philadelphia the numbers quickly dwindled to the point where the idea of splitting up the team was abandoned.

By the end of 1986, The Road Warriors were firmly back in the tag team ranks and headlined Starrcade 86 in a scaffold match against the Midnight Express. The scaffold match was an innovation of Dusty Rhodes and one of the stupidest ideas for a gimmick match I've ever seen. The idea is that instead of both teams wrestling in the ring, they are suspended above the ring on a scaffolding, and whoever pushes their opponents off first wins. How bad an idea this was became apparent when manager Jim Cornette fell off the scaffold and bodyguard Big Bubba (Ray Traylor) failed to catch him, which resulted in Cornette blowing out both knees and having injuries in both legs to date. Hawk himself worked the match on a broken ankle and showed no ill effects, but he was likely on painkillers and felt nothing. The match also had some fantastic build-up promos which included a famous one of the Warriors throwing pumpkins (representing the Express) off a balcony to the street below to show what would happen to their opponents.

Hawk's drug problems were showing themselves at this point, as his roid rages were uncontrollable and he would get into fights with opponents, fans, or anyone who was dumb enough to get in his way when the drugs kicked in. Bill Watts has a particularly grim take on Hawk's state of mind at the time:

> Hawk once told me that when he was shooting straight monkey hormones that the first thing each morning when he awoke, he wanted to kill someone. What a life.

Through 1987, the Warriors were the hottest act in the NWA and a bidding war between Jim Crockett and Vince McMahon was the result—and after losing that war (an unheard of thing at that point), Vince got revenge by creating his own version of the Road Warriors with Demolition. Ironically, Barry Darsow pops up again in this story, this time going from a Russian to Smash. Meanwhile, the Road Warriors anchored a good gimmick match for once—the Wargames. Another Dusty Rhodes invention, this one consisted of two teams of five in a double-ring cage match, with tons of blood and submission the only way to win. It was an instant smash hit and sold out arenas across the country. The Warriors' hot streak built up to a title challenge of the Horsemen's tag champions—Tully Blanchard and Arn Anderson—in Chicago, the hometown of the Warriors, at Starrcade 87, the biggest show of the year where all the babyfaces traditionally went over. And they did the Dusty Finish again, leaving the Warriors without the belts and killing the city forever.

Showing once again that no one in wrestling ever learns from past mistakes, Dusty Rhodes got it into his head to turn the Road Warriors heel again at the end of 1988, despite the AWA having tried that with no luck. The company was already on the verge of death, and Dusty turned them with a spectacular betrayal in a six-man tag match, in which the Warriors first abandoned their young partner Sting and then brutalized Dusty soon after. I use the term "brutalize" pretty loosely sometimes, but in this case it's warranted. Dusty was left so bloodied and pulverized after a spike in the eye that it nearly got Crockett's dying promotion tossed off TBS and resulted in the firing of Dusty Rhodes as booker. And still the fans wouldn't boo the Road Warriors. They finally won the NWA World tag titles from the babyface champions, the Midnight Express, on October 29 of that year, and nearly left them in the hospital and made them out to be heroic fighters until the end, and fans still wouldn't boo the Road Warriors. After months of Crockett trying everything in his power to get people not to like the Warriors, he finally gave up and turned them back again, and the Warriors dropped the tag titles to the Varsity Club in one of the screwiest finishes of all time on April 2, 1989, but the damage was done. They were no longer special, there weren't any strong heel teams left for them, and the new bureaucrats who had inherited WCW from Jim Crockett at the beginning of 1989 wanted nothing to do with their huge contract. So it was off to the WWF, which was the worst thing possible for someone with Hawk's problems.

The newly named Legion of Doom (Vince McMahon wanted nothing to do with a name created by someone else) was a pretty big deal in the tag team ranks but weren't considered main event wrestlers like they were in the NWA. They steamrolled through "imposters" Demolition (who were by far the superior team in the ring and had since become a completely different type of team than the Warriors regardless of their initial purpose) and won the WWF World tag titles from the Nasty Boys at Summerslam 91, but it just didn't feel right to anyone. This was a kinder, gentler Legion of Doom, who substituted family-friendly catch phrases like "Awwww, what a rush" in place of Hawk musing about waking up with a rat gnawing on his arm. And things got even worse for them. Despite being the hottest team in the promotion, they were mysteriously ordered to drop the tag team titles in February 1992 to the makeshift team of Ted Dibiase and IRS—and at a house show no less. They agreed on the condition that footage never be shown on TV; immediately after doing so, Hawk was suspended for failing a steroid test. They returned in time to get their win back over the team now dubbed Money Inc at Summerslam 92 (although the Natural Disasters had won the tag titles in the interim so they weren't up for grabs in that match), and immediately afterward Hawk was suspended again for steroids. Feeling he was being persecuted, Hawk freaked out and quit, or was fired, it's not clear which. Animal claimed that he was injured and his career was over, and he started collecting insurance money, which became quite the scam in wrestling for the next few years. And that seemed to be it for the Road Warriors.

Hawk bounced around with the Hell's Angels for the rest of 1992, and then returned to Japan to seek his fortunes there. Because the Warriors had burned their bridges with All Japan—their previous employer overseas—Hawk gave New Japan a call. He offered to form a new version of the Road Warriors, based on his (and everyone else's) assumption that Animal's "career-ending injury" meant that he was free to find another partner. Kensuke Sasaki was chosen as his partner, but "The New Road Warriors" only served to deepen the rift between Hawk and Animal, as apparently Animal's definition of "career ending" meant that he might return later. You can see why Lloyd's of London stopped paying out policies to wrestlers. To keep the peace, Hawk and Sasaki were renamed the Hell Raisers (also known in snarkier circles as "The Hell Roiders") and were essentially allowed to run roughshod over the NJPW tag division for the better part of a year. In fact, much like the problem faced in their initial run in the U.S., they were booked to be so dominant that there were no heel teams left with any credibility. So in a very odd move by Japanese standards, they actually assembled an even worse team to defeat them—the Jurassic Powers, comprised of Scott Norton and Hercules Hernandez. Great name, horrid workers. This led to crazy U.S.-style booking to protect the Hell Raisers, which included things like DQs and foreign objects that just weren't traditionally done in Japan. Finally, the inevitable return of Animal to Japan meant the end of the Hell Raisers, and back to the States they went in 1995 to appear on the early days of WCW Monday Nitro as the reunited Legion of Doom.

By this time, the team was clearly well past its expiration date and Eric Bischoff was hesitant (correctly, in my opinion) to offer them anything special to wrestle for WCW again. Hawk was given another shot as a single that went nowhere, and finally a frustrated Legion of Doom quietly quit again and went back to the WWF for one last try. But clearly that promotion had passed them by as well. They were used on a nostalgia run for most of 1997 and won the tag belts one last time from the Godwinns. However, they were obviously past their prime and no longer the hip thing. They quickly became the punchline to a series of jokes by the up-and-coming Degeneration X rather than the fearsome killers they used to be. Their low point came with Hawk having his trademark Mohawk shaved off as part of an angle, and they quietly dropped the titles to the hot new team of the New Age Outlaws before disappearing again. The WWF took one last shot at freshening them up in 1998, they redesigned their outfits and dubbed them "LOD 2000." But rather than a legitimate attempt to redefine the team for the new "Attitude" era, it was merely a vehicle to get rid of the increasingly embarrassing Hawk and swap Darren "Droz" Drozdov into the team instead. In one of the more questionable moral moves of the company, they ran an angle where Hawk "attempted suicide" while supposedly high on something by jumping off the Titan Tron in order to write him out of the company. But the public jabs at his drunkenness and degenerating behavior ignored the much sadder truth about his last days.

By 2000, with his career essentially over and the mighty Road Warriors reduced to doing one-shot deals for indy promotions, Hawk found Jesus, but with his liver and kidneys already long destroyed by years of abuse, it seemed too little, too late. In 2003, the WWE gave them a tryout match on live TV against the tag team champions of Rob Van Dam & Kane, but Hawk no-sold a chokeslam and didn't win himself any points for doing so. They were denied a job, and Hawk died a few months later. Animal, showing what a class act he was, returned to the WWE in 2005 and formed "The New Legion of Doom" (the third such kick at that particular can, following 1992's Crush & Animal and 1998's Droz & Animal) with the god-awful John Heidenreich, and they actually won the Smackdown version of the tag titles to really spit on Hawk's grave. Both were released in 2006, because Animal had fulfilled his purpose of doing a Road Warriors DVD and was no longer needed. But that's the business, as Hawk knew only so well. In the end, steroids were neither confirmed nor denied as the cause of his heart attack, but they certainly were a factor, along with his other damaged organs. In the end, Hawk served two valuable lessons about the world of wrestling: Party in moderation and learn to accept when it's time to let the next generation take over. Sadly, he paid no attention to either lesson.

Curt Hennig

Died February 10, 2003, of a heart attack caused by cocaine. At least it wasn't an overdose. Just hearing the name "Mr. Perfect" conjures up nostalgic memories for us fans of the '80s scene, but hearing that name increasingly conjures up the tragedy that ended his life and drowns out the good times. But that happens a lot.

The son of near-legend Larry "The Ax" Hennig, Curt was a star performer as a high school wrestler and was a natural to get ushered into the pro world by his father. A skinny jobber, Curt debuted for the AWA in 1980, but Larry Hennig smartly realized that the AWA had room for only one prodigal son at that point and sent him on a brief tour of the WWF before he ended up in Oregon in 1982 to work with Don Owen. Curt became a star when he won the PNW title in 1983, and a tour of Japan in 1985 made him into a top-level star by the time he returned to the AWA.

It was there that he truly fulfilled much of his potential and was pushed as the top contender to Nick Bockwinkel's World title, primarily because everyone else had left. The two had a spectacular five-star classic bloodbath on ESPN that ran a full sixty minutes and left fans thinking in no uncertain terms that Hennig was the biggest star in the promotion, and the biggest babyface at that. However, what the fans didn't understand, and what Verne did, was that deep down they really wanted to cheer for Verne's son Greg Gagne, who he had been unsuccessfully pushing at the top for the previous decade. I hope my sarcasm came through there. Anyway, in May 1987, they finally put the World title on Curt in a strangely booked match. The idea was that Nick Bockwinkel and Hennig would go out and have a long, good match to headline the SuperClash II show (which was a super bomb, barely filling the lower rows of seats in the arena), wherein Bockwinkel would frustrate the younger challenger by outsmarting his scientific wrestling prowess. The fans would then rally behind the older champion and his wily ways, until the young punk Hennig was forced to use a roll of coins given to him by presumed enemy Larry Zbyszko to knock Bockwinkel out and win the title by nefarious means. This tactic would act as Hennig's heel turn (so as not to threaten Greg Gagne's place in the promotion) and then they'd overturn the decision like always and give it back to Bock-winkel.

However, things turned out much different. Because Hennig was perceived as the bigger star at that point, fans actually rallied behind him during the match instead of Bockwinkel, and gave him a loud, positive reaction when he won the title. Verne Gagne then changed his mind and kept the title on him to push an epic showdown between Curt Hennig and Greg Gagne for the belt. No, really. They built the match for months, but it barely drew 2,000 people in the AWA's home city of Minneapolis. And they still didn't learn their lesson, as it ended with Gagne winning the title, only to have it overturned later, which is the same finish that killed the territory in the first place. Things were so bad for the AWA at that point that the WWF was essentially able to walk in and sign Hennig while he was still the champion, which necessitated a quickie title change to Jerry Lawler in 1988, as Hennig was literally on TV with the WWF a week afterward. Although I blame the WWF and Vince McMahon in particular for killing many territories and signing many champions who he shouldn't have, the AWA was self-destructing with or without him, and he basically saved Hennig from going down with the ship.

And so in June 1988, Curt Hennig debuted in the WWF with little fanfare but with an enlarged frame thanks to roids and was immediately repackaged in one of the most brilliant gimmick debuts ever. He was dubbed Mr. Perfect and to build up that image they shot a series of vignettes showing him doing a series of tasks, well, perfectly. The trick was simple but tortuous: If they wanted to show him swishing a basketball through a hoop from behind his back, they'd just set up the shot, get him to start shooting, and keep doing re takes until he hit it. Sometimes it would take a hundred takes, but the end result left him looking like a superstar. Coupled with an undefeated streak that stretched from his debut in 1988 until a loss to WWF champion Hulk Hogan at the end of 1989, he was clearly being positioned as a top-level star.

Hennig was a unique worker at that point for the WWF because he was a heel who was not only technically proficient, in the mold of Ted Dibiase, but also took some of the craziest bumps ever seen. He was famous for taking overblown, spinning falls off simple moves and turned getting thrown over the top rope into an art form. It seemed to be impossible to have a bad match with him, simply because he would go out and throw himself all over the ring like a ragdoll until he got a good match out of someone by sheer will power. Besides being famous for his tactics in the ring, he was also renowned for his jokes outside the ring, most notably instigating the real-life feud between Dynamite Kid and Jacques Rougeau after he cut Jacques' clothes to ribbons and then laid the blame on the British Bulldogs. He pulled a more infamous stunt when he got to WCW and while waiting under the ring to take part in an angle with Ultimate Warrior, he shit all over the floor. Kind of a commentary on the storyline, I suppose.

Hennig ascended the ladder in the WWF through 1989 and became the top contender to Hulk Hogan's WWF title, despite the presence of the ineffectual Lanny "The Genius" Poffo. Really, Hennig's already Perfect, why would he need a Genius? The feud with Hogan was memorable for quite a few reasons, though. It mainly played out on *Saturday Night's Main Event* in the early part of 1990, although their first match was at a house show and ended Hennig's year-long undefeated streak. In one of the few jobs that Hogan ever did on TV, manager Poffo wrestled Hogan on SNME and scored a now-legendary countout victory with interference from Hennig. Following that win, Hennig and Poffo stole the championship belt and smashed it with a hammer. Someone with a sense of humor not only kept that ruined belt, but taped it up eight years later and turned it into the Hardcore title in a nice nod to history. They moved onto a tag team match at the next edition of SNME that featured Hogan & Ultimate Warrior vs. Poffo & Hennig in a match that was not only one of the highest-rated wrestling matches in history but set up Hogan verses Warrior for Wrestlemania VI, one of the biggest-drawing shows in wrestling history.

After unceremoniously losing the feud to Hogan and then again losing to Hogan's BFF Brutus Beefcake at Wrestlemania, it was time to overhaul Mr. Perfect again. The Genius was out as manager, and Bobby Heenan was in to truly give him the aura of a top-level heel instead of a midcard comedy act. Hennig won the Intercontinental title vacated by Warrior's World title win by defeating Tito Santana in a tournament final taped before some of the first-round matches even aired, which is another one of those things that only happen in wrestling. The natural progression of things was to drop the title to the rapidly improving Beefcake at Summerslam 90, but fate intervened and Beefcake's face was shattered in a parasailing accident. Kerry Von Erich was brought in as the big surprise to take Beefcake's place, but by that point Kerry had self-destructed thanks to drugs and a missing foot, and even a miracle worker like Curt Hennig could only do so much with him. Although Von Erich won the title in a short match, everyone immediately realized the looming disaster as Von Erich was put on suicide watch while still holding the belt and having horrible matches on the house show circuit. The plug was pulled in November and Hennig got the title back, with the plan being a big loss to Bret Hart to turn Bret into the next superstar.

Unfortunately, the prime of Hennig's career was also his prime time for injuries, as the crazy bumps he took in every match accumulated and resulted in serious back problems for him. Hennig spent most of the first half of 1991 out of action, but either way the WWF was all too happy to advertise him for title defenses. Although he could barely drag himself to the ring for squash matches on TV, they could at least pretend he was going to be at shows around the country. Despite a back injury so crippling that he could barely make it to the ring, he still managed to have a classic, twenty-minute four-and-a-quarter star match with Bret Hart at Summerslam 91 that dropped the title clean in the middle of the ring and launched Bret's career into the stratosphere. Hennig, always playing the heel role to the hilt, stumbled back to the dressing room a broken man and seemed to drift quietly into retirement. He assumed a role as Ric Flair's "executive consultant" (i.e., manager) and started collecting a Lloyd's of London payout for his back injury. Apparently, like Animal, "retirement" was a relative thing with back injuries, because by the end of 1992 all the top faces had been fired due to steroids and Vince needed a big star on top again. And so Mr. Perfect returned, teamed with Randy Savage at Survivor Series 92, and beat former friend Ric Flair to send him back to WCW. And then, as he was falling down the card thanks to a stale gimmick, he developed another career-ending back injury and started collecting insurance payments again.

After two more years on the shelf as an off-and-on announcer and his insurance payments running out, he returned to active duty at the end of 1996. Hennig revived his heel character by "mentoring" Hunter Hearst Helmsley and costing him matches. The intention was to teach a valuable lesson to all the kids out there about the downside of paying more attention to the poontang at ringside than the opponents in the ring. Ten years later, Hunter shoved this lesson back in everyone's face by getting the biggest push of his career when he married the boss's daughter, so shame on us, I guess. Anyway, Marc Mero got involved and they did a pretty good rating by turning Hennig officially heel on him in a big angle that saw Helmsley win his first Intercontinental title. This outcome was all well and good, but Hennig was still telling Lloyd's that he was "permanently disabled," which was increasingly at odds with his involvement in onscreen action and his negotiations with the WWF to return to the ring. Finally, the insurance company blinked first and cancelled his policy and, in fact, has refused to insure wrestlers since. Hennig blamed Vince McMahon and jumped ship to WCW, leaving them with a hot angle and no payoff. Although to be fair, Hennig never actually *said* he was coming back to wrestle, he just let them infer it, much like Vince never actually tells anyone to take steroids.

So after a bidding war that drove an already paranoid McMahon even battier, Hennig chose the WCW and debuted in a nothing role as DDP's tag team partner in a mystery role that was the farthest thing from a mystery. For a brief period the WCW put him into the Four Horsemen, which was better known as being the butt of a parody by the New World Order than by anything the Horsemen did as a group. Hennig took over Arn Anderson's "spot" as Flair's number one guy and enforcer, and after the nWo mocked them it set up a WarGames match at the Fall Brawl PPV where you'd think that the Horsemen would get gloriously bloody retribution. Nope. Because WCW was all about the heel swerves at that point, Curt Hennig joined the nWo in a role about eighteen rungs down the ladder instead of a top-level position with the Horsemen, and he then won the U.S. title from Mongo McMichael for his only major title run in the company.

Hennig lost the U.S. title to DDP at Starrcade 97, the biggest show in company history, and much like the company itself it was all downhill from there for him. He did a series of jobs to up-and-coming superhero Bill Goldberg, but he had little name value left. His most fondly remembered stint came in 1999 as the company fell apart, and stemmed from a backward angle where rapper Master P would come into the southern-based company and supposedly be a babyface by preaching the virtues of gangsta rap. The comedy heels were Curt Hennig and the West Texas Rednecks (Barry Windham, Kendall Windham, and Bobby Duncum Jr.), who sang a campy refrain called "I Hate Rap" and suddenly found themselves with a revival of their careers. As usual, WCW had no idea what to do with them and they quickly faded away, which left Hennig a goofy midcard jobber again. The Vince Russo era saw Shawn Stasiak being given Hennig's old "Perfect" gimmick to supposedly get him over as the next generation of the character, but Stasiak was such a disaster as a wrestler that no one bought it for a second. Vince Russo's time in the company also led to a "retirement" angle for Hennig, who was an enemy of on-screen boss Russo and was punished by having every match be a retirement match—if he ever lost by pinfall or submission, his career was finished. So he started winning a series of matches by fluke means, again reviving his career in the most ass-backwards way possible, before he lost to Buff Bagwell at the horrendous Mayhem PPV in Toronto. Fans in attendance, who were mainly old-school WWF fans, treated him like a star for the first time in years, chanting "Perfect" to rally him before he lost. And then they applauded him like a hero because he was retiring.

He returned the next night on *Nitro*, working for Vince Russo as a heel, and the whole thing was forgotten by everyone.

By 2002, with the WCW long dead and Hennig mainly doing one-shot deals like the god-awful startup promotion called the XWF, he was kinda sorta becoming a star again. He was pushed as the XWF's main heel, had a decent '80s-style match with Hulk Hogan in the main event of their first taping, and even lured Bobby Heenan out of retirement to manage him. So it shouldn't have come as too huge a surprise when he was announced as a participant in the Royal Rumble, but it was a pretty big surprise anyway. It proved more surprising to the XWF, who suddenly had no top heel and folded soon thereafter. Hennig started what looked like a nostalgia run, but it was obvious he had nothing left in the tank. After getting into a fight with Brock Lesnar on a flight home from England and nearly killing everyone on board by running into the door, he was fired with no double-dealing or pretenses this time around.

Hennig's death, which was caused by cocaine sending his heart into arrest, was precipitated by years of steroid use that had enlarged his heart to dangerous size. These circumstances foreshadowed the death of Eddie Guerrero. However, because Hennig didn't have the good fortune to die while under WWE contract, they simply mourned him with a graphic on their TV show and didn't bother to ask themselves, for instance, whether his years of steroid use in the WWF possibly had anything to do with his death. It wouldn't have saved him, but it might have saved Eddie and possibly Benoit as well.

Miss Elizabeth

Died from acute toxicity caused by an accidental drug overdose of painkillers and vodka on May 1, 2003. Really, the lovely and demure star of the '80s was the last person you'd expect to come to a fairly ugly end like that, but it just goes to show that wrestling can chew up and spit out even the nicest people. From a groundbreaking symbol of female empowerment to shacking up with Lex Luger, Miss Elizabeth's death is another one that makes me sad to think about, so I try to avoid it. Even worse, Luger was then arrested for the gigantic quantities of drugs he had around the house, which really cast a shadow on her memory.

Her success in the '80s was as unexpected and unlikely as any story to come out of wrestling. As a teenage fan of Randy Savage in Kentucky, she regularly attended the ICW shows where Randy was a local star and turned herself into a looker in order to win him away from female wrestler Debbie Combs. She became part of the business and they were married in 1984, which resulted in Elizabeth having a small part on the weekly TV show doing interviews. However, ICW was a money loser that was getting beaten regularly by Jerry Jarrett's Memphis promotion, and it was obvious that Randy Savage was far too big a star to be anywhere but the World Wrestling Federation. And thus Elizabeth came with him and got her first real big role on TV, as his shy and demure manager. But it wasn't supposed to be that way. Savage's debut had come with a big running angle (later copied with Bam Bam Bigelow) where all the heel managers were bidding for his services and all of them thought they had won them. The angle worked because all the managers were largely interchangeable at that point—I mean really, once the bell rang it didn't matter if it was Freddie Blassie or Mr. Fuji out there—and when Savage shocked everyone by announcing that Elizabeth would be managing him, it was the total opposite of the normal dynamic for a manager. Here was this polite, dignified, and quiet woman who looked like a movie star and didn't appear to be evil at all. The original plan, as was evident by her very early interviews on shows like *Tuesday Night Titans*, was for her to reveal herself as a conniving bitch and take control of his career. But the niceness just shone through (that itself was a rarity for wrestling) and fans took to the original form of the character. The WWF rolled with it and turned Savage into the maniacally jealous boyfriend who would kill anyone that looked at his woman the wrong way.

In retrospect, she was a brilliant foil for Savage once she got her character down, because he was such an over-the-top loony that fans couldn't help but cheer for him. Why? Confidence sells tickets. Say what you will about gimmicks or pushing the right people or the look or whatever, but stick someone out there who believes he's the best and can deliver that in a promo, and people will get behind him and treat him like a star. And if there was one thing that Savage had buckets of, it was confidence. However, putting him with Elizabeth meant that he instantly had a weak spot that turned him into a raving, jealous boyfriend who people wouldn't possibly want to cheer. Left to his own devices, he'd shoot up the ranks to World champion, but with Elizabeth the character became much more interesting because you never knew when he'd get sidetracked or distracted, and that's where he gained his second dimension as a character.

However, there was a darker side to their relationship. Savage's cartoonish jealousy on screen when faced with cartoonish characters like George "The Animal" Steele masked his real-life cartoonish jealousy about his wife. He was notorious for locking her in the dressing room and paying people to guard her while he was away and attacking fans who touched her on the way to the ring. But despite his insanity and well-documented drug use, he held it together well enough for the couple to become one of the biggest drawing acts of the '80s. His matches with Hulk Hogan were huge hits, and Elizabeth, who played the role of the normal person stuck in the circus of wrestling, was one of the few stars in the business that fans seemed to legitimately care about. Although in reality she also played a cartoonish role—the beautiful girl next door who would talk to the ugly guys and wasn't a stuck up bitch. The hook was that she was attainable as a person, but ultimately unattainable because she was with such a psychopathically jealous boyfriend. And that made people feel all the more sympathetic for her and made Randy Savage that much more of a star. It was a brilliant act, really.

By late 1987, Savage was over so huge that the inevitable occurred and people began cheering for him, especially once he lost the Intercontinental title to Ricky Steamboat in their classic match at Wrestlemania III. It made him look human and beatable again, and once people feel sympathy for a heel, you might as well turn him babyface—which they did in spectacular fashion. Elizabeth had never gotten physically involved before, but following a match on *Saturday Night's Main Event* that Savage had with new I-C champion Honky Tonk Man where he won by disqualification, her status suddenly changed. Savage won the battle, but Honky tried to win the war by teaming up with stablemates the Hart Foundation and attacking Savage. Liz intervened and got shoved to the mat, which broke her shoulder strap. Mild stuff, to be sure, but this was a huge shock to fans who had never seen anyone lay a hand on her before. But she proved to be not only beautiful but also smart by retrieving Hulk Hogan from the dressing room (hey, might as well get the biggest and best guy in the promotion to make the save, right?) and forming the MegaPowers (aka The Down Payment on Vince's New Yacht) to avenge her. The two biggest faces in the wrestling world, Hogan and Savage were now teamed up and fans started choosing sides right away. You could just smell the money being printed.

Savage won the WWF World title at Wrestlemania IV after what felt like an eighteen-hour tournament, and the image of Liz on his shoulders holding the belt is one of those iconic moments from wrestling history. She also became more involved as Savage was on top of the promotion, with the focus of Summerslam 88 being around her involvement at ringside and the possibility of her showing up in a bikini to distract the heels if need be. As it turned out, it was only the bottom half of one, but then Vince Russo wasn't booking at that point. But don't worry, the soap opera would come soon enough. Specifically, it came at the second live *The Main Event* show on NBC in February 1989, with Savage's jealous character rearing its ugly (but awesome) head again. During a crappy match with Big Bossman & Akeem, Elizabeth got wiped out at ringside by a flying Savage, which was especially shocking because she had never even taken a bump before. Selfish jerk Hogan carried her back to the dressing room and gave us some Daytime Emmy Award winning acting (after asking for a time countdown on live TV . . . whoops), and left Savage to get beat up by the heels for another five minutes. What a role model. Savage, upset about being abandoned and seeing his woman in the arms of another man, or maybe just really disgusted with Hogan's horrible acting, went nuts even by his standards, threatening to kill his wife and Hogan and basically cutting the heel promo of seventeen lifetimes while turning back into the monster lunatic bloodthirsty madman we all know and love.

Hogan won the eventual match at Wrestlemania V and got the girl, while Savage got Sherri Martell, the only person who could match his lunacy. Elizabeth's role essentially filled, and wanting to start a family and get away from the circus of wrestling, she disappeared for a good long while. My question would be: Did she really think Randy Savage was going to be the kind of guy to walk away from the business quietly? Elizabeth returned in 1990 for a one-shot deal at ringside for a comedy match at Wrestlemania VI between Dusty Rhodes and Randy Savage that involved their valets, but other than that she remained out of the limelight. By 1991, their marriage was falling apart and in one of those bizarre things you get only in wrestling, they thought it would be a really good idea to work things out by revealing their true relationship to the wrestling world and doing a marriage angle to reignite things. It started well enough with Savage losing a retirement match to Ultimate Warrior at Wrestlemania VII and facing the wrath of his manager Sherri. Elizabeth had been shown at ringside watching with concern, and she ran into the ring and made the save for Savage, chasing off a clearly PMS-ing Sherri. Female fans in the audience cried as they reunited (and men all had dust in their eyes or something . . .), and it was probably one of the most wonderfully scripted moments in the promotion's history, because it fed on real emotion and was a moment that fans had been literally waiting for for years. This reconciliation led to the inevitable wedding at Summerslam 91 and, because it's a wrestling wedding, the reception was crashed by Jake Roberts and Undertaker. This brought Savage out of retirement for a pretty great series of matches with the Snake, and it led to Savage getting the WWF World title back for an unlikely second reign, which began at Wrestlemania VIII.

Another huge angle involved Elizabeth. Champion Ric Flair famously braged that "she was mine before she was yours," and used Photoshopped pictures of them together that implied a previous romantic entanglement. He also promised a giant naked picture of Elizabeth to distract Savage during their title match, which was never delivered and never mentioned again. The whole episode, however, foreshadowed the direction that the entire promotion would go in years later when such gimmicks became commonplace—sometimes occurring two or three times in the same show. And the naked pictures were always delivered.

Although the Flair program was good money for the WWF in 1992, Elizabeth had had enough of the business and the marriage, as Savage had gotten increasingly crazier and more possessive over the years. She divorced Savage in September 1992 and left the promotion and wrestling, seemingly for good. Savage's on-screen claims of "lust" by Hulk Hogan in 1989 were soon echoed in real life when he accused Hogan of breaking up his marriage, and they never truly reconciled despite their on-screen "friendship" in WCW later on. For her part, Elizabeth seemed to want a normal life again, and she quickly hooked up with a lawyer in Florida, who she married in 1997 and took a job selling clothes at a mall.

But in 1996, for whatever reason, Elizabeth decided to call WCW looking for work again. She was paired with Ric Flair for a super-hot program with Randy Savage that ignited the company shortly before the New World Order would send it into orbit, but things just weren't the same. She tried to play the devil-woman character that the WWF had originally wanted her to be, but it just wasn't her. She became a target of derision by the WWF, as a silly spot with her shoe as a weapon was turned into an entire skit on RAW as part of the Billionaire Ted fiasco. After the Flair thing ran its course, she became a plaything of the nWo, standing around in the background and applauding for Hogan and Eric Bischoff. Elizabeth was repackaged with Randy Savage when he joined the nWo, but even a hot feud with Diamond Dallas Page couldn't make fans buy her as the evil companion for the Macho Man. By 1998, she had largely disappeared from the TV shows again, and was not-so-secretly cheating on her husband with Lex Luger in real life. In her last major role in wrestling, she was paired with him when he was reinvented as The Total Package in 1999. Elizabeth became a fitness nut herself, and turned her aging and slightly frumpy body into a more toned look again. It didn't work because she was little more than eye candy but looked, to be frank, old.

After WCW folded in 2001 and it was apparent that Luger was blackballed from the WWF for screwing them over in 1995, Elizabeth largely disappeared again, doing only occasional shows as Luger's manager. Despite their talk of getting married and having a family, things were not as happy with them as they appeared. By 2003, and out of the spotlight for two years and largely forgotten by the new generation of fans, Luger was having a rough time with semi-retirement and had turned to a virtual pharmacy at home to medicate himself. Luger and Elizabeth seemingly hit bottom as a couple when police responded to a domestic dispute call at their home and arrested Luger for battery, and then two days later arrested him again for DUI.

> I was a heartbeat away. I almost overdosed probably dozens of times. I had a really fast metabolism. Part of why Lex stayed so lean wasn't just drugs. God blessed me with a very fast metabolism. I metabolized drugs quickly. That is not good, but it saved my life a bunch of times. I went in deep a bunch of times with pills and alcohol. I was a pill-popper. And I abused alcohol toward the end, real bad. I take a lot of responsibility for that—my influence in her life. Her little heart and body couldn't take what I was doing.*

The pathetic 911 call that Luger made on the day Elizabeth died was played on WWE TV as a sad reminder that no one, not even the grieving, are allowed to escape with dignity intact after leaving. Luger was portrayed as a coward who allowed her to die, one last cheap shot taken by the company who wouldn't hire him again in the first place. As another slap in his face, police found more than 1,000 illegal pills in their home and arrested him a third time for felony narcotics possession. Having finally hit bottom in 2006 after going to jail for parole violation, he found religion and seemingly has turned his life around, long after he can do any good for the business and long after Elizabeth paid the price for his previous habits. After her death, Jim "Ultimate Warrior" Hellwig actually raised a good point about Savage's treatment of her:

*sports.espn.go.com/espn/print?id=3016179&type=story

I knew the Elizabeth the whole world knew—she was Randy's wife. Few talent—if that many—ever got closer to her than that while they were married. Randy was very protective of her and did not allow a line leading to over-friendly contact. And, believe me, the lines Randy drew never had slack in them. He knew full-well too many talent in the business had no scruples so he never subjected his beloved to the chance. Let there be no mistake—wound up as the "Macho" element of Randy's life was, when it came to his marriage he was disciplined and controlled, had class and respected it traditionally.*

Would Elizabeth still be alive if she was sheltered from the business like a delicate flower at all times? Probably, and that's kind of scary in a way. She was different from all the others who followed; but in the end, she was just the same, and that's the saddest thing about it.

Crash Holly

Michael "Crash Holly" Lockwood died on November 6, 2003, of the usual drug overdose. He had a long independent career as Erin O'Grady, an Irish character, but it was his stint in the WWE as Crash Holly, wannabe super-heavyweight, that earned him his greatest degree of fame.

In 1999 a tape that featured his matches with Vic Grimes made it to WWF offices, and although both wrestlers were brought in, only Lockwood was signed. Due to his resemblance to Hardcore Holly he was turned into Holly's "cousin" Crash, who had a size hangup and carried a scale with him to prove that he was bigger than his stature indicated. On a more serious note, he was obviously a heavy steroid

*www.misselizabeth.com/extra/interview10.html

user, despite his reputation as a health nut, and turned his light-weight frame into a far more muscled one in an echo of his character. The Hollys had a brief run as the WWF World tag team champions in 1999 despite their frequent fights with each other, but it wasn't until Crash was introduced into the Hardcore division that his career took off. In a strange gimmick that was one of the few truly new ideas left in wrestling, Crash won the Hardcore title from Test in 2000 and offered to defend it anytime, anywhere. This stipulation led to the belt having a de facto "24/7 Rule," which meant that whoever was champion was fair game to defend his belt whenever challenged for it. Although an effective idea in the short term, the gimmick wore out its welcome once everyone in the promotion had won the belt, and the entire Hardcore division was shut down in 2002.

Crash went on to win the European title while on tour, and won it from and lost it back to William Regal, but it was obvious that his character had run its course in the promotion. He was fired in 2003 and went to TNA as Mad Mikey. Perhaps this was a true-to-life gimmick, because he was having marriage problems at the time and was quite upset about it, which led to an overdose that was timed suspiciously enough so that it could be thought of as suicide. In another example of the problems within wrestling, Crash's addictions were no secret when he was fired by WWE in 2003, but TNA picked him up immediately.

Louie Spicolli

Louis Mucciolo, who was more popularly known as Louie Spicolli in the U.S., died on February 27, 1998, while employed by WCW and in the midst of the biggest push of his career. Louie was only twenty-seven at the time, one of the most poignant examples of how the sport can destroy lives before they really get started. He had been a fan of the WWF all his life, and after leaving school he trained to be a wrestler, starting as a TV jobber for the WWF at age seventeen.

With that career going nowhere, he quit and wrestled for AAA in Mexico, where he bulked up and adopted the silly Madonna's Boyfriend persona as a part of a team with Eddie Guerrero and Art Barr of invading "Los Gringos Locos." Of course, all three members would be dead by 2005.

In yet another unspoken approval of the steroid mindset by the WWF, they saw the AAA/WCW *When Worlds Collide* PPV show and immediately signed Spicolli to a new deal, citing his increased size and weight (thanks to . . . what else?) as the reason for giving him another shot. In this case, Spicolli bulked up because he thought that's what they wanted, and he was immediately proved right. He was saddled with a loser gimmick, however, playing "grunge rocker" Rad Radford in 1995, long after the Seattle craze had run its course in pop culture. By the end of the year, he was tagging along with the Bodydonnas (Chris "Skip" Candido and Tammy "Sunny" Sytch) and trying out for a spot with them in a storyline that made no sense. The first serious problems in his life came during that gimmick, as he overdosed on Soma and was found passed out on his neighbor's lawn. The WWF pretty much fired him on the spot, and he ended up in ECW. Although Paul Heyman gave him a big push because of his rising name and indy cred, his drug problems were out of control and he was gone again by 1997. No one was even trying to help him at that point and the only promotion dumb enough to take another chance on him was WCW.

WCW was his last career move, and he was essentially a TV jobber for a few weeks until a friendship with Scott Hall led to a gig playing his "caddy," in a role based on comedian Chris Farley. Spicolli was used in a comic relief role that got over so effectively he was given tryouts as a color commentator in his last days. Although he had supposedly kicked the worst of his drug habits, the WCW atmosphere at that point was a constant party, and he got swept away in it. His next overdose would be his last, and he was found dead in the home of friend Steven Richards. His autopsy later found twenty-six Somas in his system, washed down with wine, a combination that he would often take to get to sleep. It was said that he could have been a professional baseball player, or anything he wanted, but he wanted to be a wrestler. More's the pity.

Junkyard Dog

Died June 1, 1998, in a car accident. It would of course be silly to blame his death directly on drugs and alcohol, although they certainly didn't help to extend his life.

For many, the death of JYD was the death of the Rock N Wrestling era of the '80s—aside from Andre the Giant, the Dog was the first big name from the true cartoon era of the WWF to die. Given the nostalgia tour that has been the careers of Roddy Piper and Hulk Hogan for the past ten years or so, JYD probably could have been headlining RAW or TNA Impact today had his career not effectively come to an end, years before his death due to the drugs. There was a certain symmetry to his life and death, however. Years earlier, Dog's daughter was born in the midst of a historic angle in Mid-South where the Freebirds "blinded" him and he was unable to witness her birth. In interviews he gave shortly before his death, he intimated that he was essentially hanging on until she fulfilled his dream for her—graduating high school. Having attended that ceremony, he was driving home when he died.

Born Sylvester Ritter, JYD was struggling for a career in the NFL and, like many failed football players, decided to give wrestling a try. He was working a tour in Germany and doing terribly at it by all accounts, but ran into Bruce Hart from Stampede Wrestling. Bruce sold his father on turning Sylvester Ritter into Big Daddy Ritter, a jive-talking, womanizing monster heel. Despite his shortcomings in the ring, Stu Hart always had a soft spot for football players, and the Harts showed Ritter the ropes enough to allow him to develop into a good draw for the promotion. However, it was when Ritter and fellow Southerner Jake Roberts defected to Bill Watts' upstart Mid-South Wrestling promotion and Ritter was dubbed The Junkyard Dog that his career really went places.

Of course, the storyline that launched him into superstardom in that area was the blinding at the hands of the Freebirds. After winning the tag team titles from the Freebirds, Hayes got his revenge by using the dreaded (and very mysterious) Freebird Cream to blind the Dog, which turned him into a local folk hero for the largely black fanbase that the Dog drew to the shows. Back in the days before the Internet would ruin this sort of experience for everyone, JYD stuck to his character by remaining in his home almost around the clock, to make sure no fans saw him without his bandages and dark glasses. In a memorable and wholly unpredictable twist to the storyline, he was going to do a "farewell speech" to the fans (which would obviously set up a Freebird attack of some sort), but a fan jumped out of the audience and pulled a gun on Michael Hayes before any such plot twist could be played out. That's the kind of dedication that JYD inspired in his fans. Not that I'm condoning it, but you've gotta admit that not many wrestlers can inspire that kind of devotion from their audience. Dog of course was miraculously "unblinded" and got his revenge in front of sold out shows around the territory.

But while his professional life was strong, his personal life was anything but. In a "chicken or the egg" type of circular origin, his marriage started falling apart, either because of or causing his increasing cocaine usage. His wife actually ended up institutionalized as a result of the breakup, so you can imagine how well it went. Dog's formerly ripped body turned into a bloated mess; and at his lowest point as a person but highest peak as a draw, the WWF signed him away without notice to Watts. It was a shock to the territory, and Watts never really recovered from it.

This began the period of the biggest stardom for JYD, and he won the first and only Wrestling Classic tournament by defeating Randy Savage by countout in the finals. He was also a featured star

at the first *Wrestlemania* in 1985 and defeated Intercontinental champion Greg Valentine by countout. However, by 1987 he was reduced
to a midcard role, dancing in the ring with kids and providing voice-
overs for his cartoon likeness as second banana on *Hulk Hogan's Rock
N Wrestling*. His last major match came at *Wrestlemania III*, putting
over "King" Harley Race in a short, bad match before getting fired
shortly after as his drug problems consumed him. His weight also
became a problem as he bounced around independent promotions
until 1990 and weighed over 330 pounds. WCW brought him back
as an opponent for Ric Flair in an effort to cut costs with name-brand
stars who worked cheap, but even this limited role was then too
much to expect from him and he was fired again soon after.

Although the drugs didn't crash his car that night, they might
as well have because he had little left to live for after losing his marriage, job, car, house, and money years earlier because of cocaine.
Oh, and remember the symmetry I mentioned earlier? While he never
got to see his daughter's birth as part of a storyline, he also never got
to see her graduation because he arrived late. That's just kind of
the way things went for him in the end. Truly a guy who had it
all and sniffed it all away, and it's really hard to sympathize with
his losses.

Big Dick Dudley

Alex Rizzo died May 16, 2002, of kidney failure. I only include him
in this list as a courtesy because he was never a star outside of a brief
run with ECW from 1996–1998. However, he had enough of a name
and was such an obvious user of steroids and self-medication that
it's worth mentioning because the link between the drugs and his
death is crystal clear. Neither of the Big Two ever wanted to bother
hiring him, although it's more likely that it was just because he was
so awful rather than any aversion to his habits.

"Ravishing" Rick Rude

Rick Rood died April 20, 1999 of a heart attack caused by a drug overdose while training for his comeback. Rood's death was another one that hurt, partially because the character of Ravishing Rick Rude was such a great heel and an integral part of fandom for myself and many others during a huge time for the business, and partially because he was a guy who hadn't been such a great worker but who ultimately worked his way up to the level he was pushed.

His origins in the sport were fairly humble. He was part of the same group of bouncers that produced the Road Warriors and Barry Darsow in Minnesota, but unlike them he had neither the unique look nor the charisma to carry him above lower-card status in his early days with Mid-South Wrestling. Although Bill Watts didn't see anything in him, Jerry Jarrett in Memphis did and pushed him as a top heel with the womanizing heel act that Rood would go on to make famous later. He also changed his name to "Ravishing Rick Rude." It has long been my contention that Ravishing Rick Rude is the best heel name in wrestling history because it wasn't dependent on ethnic stereotyping in the way of more traditional Japanese or German heel names. More importantly, it had all the qualities that great wrestling names have: Alliteration, short syllables that fans can chant easily, and an expression of his basic character without ever having to hear him talk. He's ravishing and he's rude, that's all you need to know. Would you cheer for him knowing that out of the gate? Of course not.

After top runs in Memphis and Florida as the guy that everyone else carried because they could make money off him and his abs, he moved to the World Class promotion in Texas and became the beneficiary of the first ever World Class World Heavyweight title when Fritz Von Erich broke away from the NWA and wanted his own World title. Oddly, instead of going to the WWF, the logical next step,

Rude jumped to the NWA instead and, almost immediately upon debuting, won the NWA World tag team titles from the Rock N Roll Express with Manny Fernandez as a partner. The team was a huge success as a heel duo, but Rude wanted to be a singles star again and finally jumped to the WWF in May 1987. However, he didn't give Jim Crockett any notice and left without dropping the tag titles. On TV they announced that stablemate Ivan Koloff would be defending the tag titles with Manny Fernandez while Rude recovered from an "injury," but then Fernandez left as well and they just threw logic completely out the window and aired an old match against the Rock N Roll Express. Thus, in one of those things that only happen in wrestling, the Rock N Roll Express regained the tag team titles by winning a match that had been taped something like five months earlier, which had happened in a city where they didn't have a show on the night that it supposedly happened.

Rude didn't exactly make a big splash on his entrance into the promotion, and primarily worked as a main event heel around the horn with Hulk Hogan. Now that sounds big, but keep in mind that this was basically a rotating spot where has-beens like Killer Khan or Kamala or Sika would come in for a few weeks, get some wins on TV to build them up, and then lose to Hogan and disappear. It was also at that point that Rude had a conversation with Vince McMahon that became the subject of some controversy in the months following Chris Benoit's death. During the Vince McMahon steroid trials of 1994, Rude was called to the stand and was the only person to ever accuse Vince of directly telling him to put on weight with steroids. He testified that Vince had told him he "didn't look good" while off the juice and should get back on it. Rude got bigger and so did his push, and his arrogant catch phrases and delivery both mesmerized and irritated female fans. In a storyline prototype that later defined the "Attitude Era," Rude had his big break chasing after Jake Roberts' wife Cheryl in a feud that was more "real" because people knew that Jake and Cheryl were really married. The feud culminated with Rude getting his tights pulled down on TV shows as payback, all of which was exactly the sort of trailer-park mentality that would be amplified in the Vince Russo booking strategy years later.

Rude remained a solid midcarder until early 1989, when he was programmed with Ultimate Warrior and suddenly improved tenfold in the ring by discovering chemistry with one of the worst main eventers of the modern era. Rude managed to work miracles and get good matches out of him, like their Intercontinental title match at *Wrestlemania V* when Rude scored the massive upset after bumping like a pinball for Warrior and gave Bobby Heenan his first champion in the WWF. This match actually did wonders for Rude's career, as he was suddenly a serious force instead of the pretty boy arrogant heel who did comedy matches. Although Warrior regained the title at *Summerslam 89* a few months later, Rude was kept on the backburner and turned into Warrior's first big program when he won the WWF World title in 1990. For his part, Rude was also repackaged to prep Warrior for his main event run. Rude was given a marine-like crewcut and an all-business attitude instead of the taunting promos he normally cut. He did good numbers on top with Warrior, but that was part of his undoing in the WWF. Although Rude injured his arm, the classy Vince McMahon continued to advertise him against Warrior in matches he had no chance of making. Rude felt quite rightly that if his name was being used to draw money then he deserved a cut of it and quit over that dispute.

WCW jumped all over Rude in 1991 and brought him in as the surprise heel at *Halloween Havoc 91* to squash Tom Zenk. They then pushed him to the moon as the anchor for their new super-stable— Paul Heyman's "Dangerous Alliance." After winning the U.S. title from Sting in a highly rated *Clash of the Champions* special, he hit the peak of his career by moving up to the NWA World title tournament finals in Japan in 1992 but losing to Masa Chono. He gained huge amounts of respect for his performance in the process, however. Rude was now a legitimate World title level worker in WCW and at the top of his game, and WCW taped future segments with him holding the NWA World title. Before I get into the numerous problems associated with future tense for stuff that was supposed to have been happening in the past and my brain explodes in the present while you're reading a book that won't be published until a year after I write it, a quick word about WCW in 1993. To cut costs and because the company was run by chimps who couldn't pick their own noses without paperwork in triplicate from the home office, WCW used to tape literally three months of programming at a time in TV studios in Orlando. Ironically, TNA moved into those studios in 2004 without a *hint* of irony, but I don't want to get sidetracked. At one of those tapings, Rick Rude did interviews while carrying the NWA World title belt (aka The Big Gold Belt), with the implication being that he had defeated Ric Flair for it at the *Fall Brawl 93* PPV show that would not yet have happened for the people in attendance. The NWA, who were no longer a part of WCW and were simply copromoting with them for the exposure, caught wind of this "title change" and pulled their support, which left WCW with weeks of taped TV and no actual title to back it up. So in a move ludicrous even by WCW's low standards, the title match was changed to simply "The Big Gold Belt," with no wrestling title implied in the name, and that's what Rude won at the PPV. Later it was changed to the "WCW International World title," which somehow sounded even dumber.

Regardless, it was the last ring title for Rude, because he dropped it to Sting in April 1994 and then seriously injured his back while regaining it in Japan. Because Rude had a large Lloyd's of London insurance policy to fall back on like best friend Curt Hennig, he chose retirement and left the business until 1997. When he got the wrestling bug again, as so many do, it was a far different business than the one he left. The WWF was no longer dominant and found itself battling for TV ratings with WCW's Monday Nitro and to a (much) lesser extent, ECW. Rude was contacted by ECW owner Paul Heyman to do color commentary for his show, as someone to offset babyface announcer Joey Styles. But Rude made a far better promo guy when confined to his "What I would like to have right now . . ." catch phrase instead of trying to tell a story on the air. So Rude was turned into the venerable Mysterious Masked Man who tormented the heels and then revealed himself as being aligned with them, and that got him hot enough again that Vince McMahon wanted him for another run. Rude's back was still shot, so he was aligned with Shawn Michaels' D-Generation X faction, the hottest act in wrestling at that point, as their "insurance policy" (aka bodyguard).

However, in the aftermath of the Montreal Screwjob, Rude sided with Bret Hart and contacted Eric Bischoff about jumping ship. This gave Rude one last historic moment, as he became the only person until then to appear on WCW Monday Nitro (clean shaven) and WWF Monday Night RAW (taped six days earlier, with a beard) on the same night. WCW played it up as a huge coup, but it was really a meaningless acquisition because Rude wasn't even working with a contract for WWE and was a disposable part of the DX stable. Rude essentially did nothing with WCW but act as a manager for the nWo and little else. Rumors began circulating in 1998 that he was suffering from testicular cancer, which was later revealed to be nothing more serious than a cyst. In fact, he was training for a comeback in the ring, assuming he could get one of the promotions to buy out his insurance policy, but a mixture of pain medications he was taking for his back problems overwhelmed him. Although no definitive answer was forthcoming from the autopsy, best guess is a lethal combination of painkillers, GHB, and steroids. It's just another case of someone who thought he had escaped, but then ended up dead like all the others because he couldn't give it up.

Big Bossman

Ray Traylor died September 22, 2004, from a massive heart attack. Ray was one of those dependable guys you could stick with whatever goofy gimmick you needed, and he'd be game for it. Obviously his greatest success was playing a prison guard but, considering the stuff that WCW made him go through (The CPAs, anyone?), it's amazing he remained as big a star as he did throughout the years.

They say the best gimmicks are the person "turned up to 11," and that was certainly the case with Ray, who was discovered by Jim Cornette while working as a prison guard in Cobb County, Georgia. Despite his extreme shyness and total lack of in-ring ability, at 330 pounds on a 6'6" frame, Traylor had an intimidating look. His physical stature was enhanced by sticking him in a suit meant to show that someone his size should not be wearing a suit, and he quickly joined the ranks of the Midnight Express as Big Bubba Rogers, bodyguard for Cornette. Traylor immediately made the right friends and became the personal project of booker Dusty Rhodes, who booked him as an unkillable bad-ass and came up with a legendary spot where Dusty would break a wooden chair over Bubba's head and Bubba would merely adjust his tie instead of showing pain. And people wonder why concussions in wrestling are a problem. At any rate, the angle worked spectacularly well and NWA fans completely bought into Bubba Rogers as a force for intimidation. Although he was perceived as a brute in the ring, in reality he was quite clumsy and oafish, which was most effectively shown at *Starrcade '86* in the famous scaffold match between the Midnight Express and the Road Warriors. In the big spot, Jim Cornette was to fall off the scaffold and into the arms of Rogers, but it went completely wrong. Jim Cornette relates the story in a shoot interview from 2000 . . .

Dusty pitched Cornette's fall as him being caught "like the guys catch the cheerleaders at the football games" by his bodyguard, Big Bubba Rogers (Big Bossman). Once they realized that wasn't going to work, Cornette and Bubba improvised Bubba grabbing Cornette on the way down then rolling to the side to break part of the fall, which they'd gotten from seeing a program on skydiving. In execution, "Bobby fell like this *woosh*. Dennis fell like this *woosh*. I fell like this *THUMP*." Bubba "lost me in the lights" and, the next thing he knew, he was seeing stars on the mat because he'd gone through Bubba's arms, screwed up his leg, and hit his head on Bubba's knee. "It was a good thing I'd gotten hit on the head because it knocked me temporarily senseless and acted as a natural anaesthetic because I thought I was gonna see a bone coming out of my leg." After that, he was speaking in falsetto and Bubba could barely hear him saying "Carry me, carry me." Bubba thought he was selling, so Cornette said "I'm shootin', I'm shootin'", which Bubba thought was "I'm shittin', I'm shittin'" because he was green. Cornette finally said "Bubba . . . CARRYMYGODDAMNASSNOW!"*

With Bill Watts' UWF (the former Mid-South Wrestling gone national) in its dying days and increasingly under the banner of Jim Crockett Promotions, the rapidly improving Traylor was sent in to hone his craft and still under the protection of Dusty Rhodes. Big Bubba, now repackaged as a singles wrestler, joined the heel "army" of manager Skandor Akbar, quickly won the UWF World title from stablemate One Man Gang before dropping it to Steve "Dr. Death" Williams after a healthy reign. Inevitably, the WWF came calling and the larger-than-life Traylor debuted in the summer of 1988 with the larger-than-life character of Big Bossman, a corrupt prison guard who dished out "justice" whether the victims deserved it or not. And with that kind of character on his back, the only place to go was up and into a feud with Hulk Hogan, in which Bossman more than carried his weight, so to speak. A famous match took place between them at the peak of their feud, on *Saturday Night's Main Event* when Boss-

*forums.thesmartmarks.com

man challenged for the title in a cage match and Hogan won after superplexing the giant Bossman from the top of the cage.

With his main event run over by 1989, he was repackaged into a tag team with former opponent One Man Gang, who was himself repackaged into Akeem the African Dream (a not-so-subtle shot at Dusty Rhodes). Throughout the course of 1989, Bossman steadily dropped weight until he was at an impressive 250 or so by 1990, just in time for his face turn. He quickly became one of the most popular characters in the WWF, and his corrupt prison guard became a modern-day cowboy fighting for justice and trying to avenge Bobby Heenan's comments about his mother. That particular feud actually led to the departure of Rick Rude from the promotion, because he was the heel who made the disparaging remarks, but he suffered an injury before the fairly hot feud could be blown off on house shows. That didn't stop the WWF from advertising him, however, and as related earlier, Rude felt that since he was drawing the houses, he should get the bigger cut of the money. Bossman quickly evolved into the premiere "big man" worker of the early '90s, and moved with uncanny speed for someone that big, thanks to his dramatic weight loss and conditioning. He became part of a party clique with Rude and Curt Hennig, which was certainly a tragic group to be associated with. He almost certainly never dabbled in steroids (I mean, look at him), but stories about his indulgences on the road were rumored at the time and long after.

His last big feud in the WWF was against goofy heel Nailz, supposedly an escaped convict from the prison where Bossman used to work. This feud played out in 1992 during an especially cartoonish period for the WWF, when Vince was distracted by steroid allegations and revenues were falling. It was supposed to build to an "electric chair" match, if you can believe it (an idea actually lifted from WCW), but Nailz was fired for a variety of reasons in November 1992, and it turned into an ugly lawsuit as he accused Vince of sexual advances. The Big Bossman, with nothing left to do in the pro-

motion, was signed by WCW in late 1993 as they began their plan
of signing anyone ever associated with the WWF. Problems immediately surfaced, however, as they wanted to call him The Boss and
have him be a police officer who carried a nightstick; but in one of
the rare instances where the WWF legal team actually won a case,
they rightly pointed out how inane an idea it was. (Especially when
WCW announcer Tony Schiavone would make "accidental" remarks
on TV like "The Boss . . . man, is he big.") Despite a string of great
matches with Vader in 1994, the Boss gimmick was dropped and
Traylor was retooled into the Guardian Angel, based on the group
of the same name. By 1995, Traylor was effectively past his prime as
a worker and suffered from lack of motivation and an increasing
painkiller problem, and he progressed through a series of lackluster
attempts to recapture the former magic he once had. They tried a
heel turn and turned him back into Big Bubba Rogers, then put him
with the nWo as Big Bubba, then turned him face as plain Ray Traylor, but by 1998 he was little more than a jobber who rarely got promo
time. This situation was best summed up by a fan's sign at ringside
at that point, which famously read "Ray Traylor: Will Job For Food."

Clearly it was time for a change, and he jumped back to the WWF
in 1998, having remained on good terms with front office personnel
and also having a ready-made gimmick waiting for him: The Big
Bossman. Now playing the bodyguard for the evil Mr. McMahon,
the Bossman was briefly reborn, although injuries and weight gain
left him a shadow of his former self in the ring. He won his first
major title in the Big Two, taking the WWF World tag titles with Ken
Shamrock in 1998, and soon became a fixture of the Hardcore division. His last years in the sport will probably be remembered for the
campy, over-the-top storylines that Vince Russo wrote for him. He
feuded with Al Snow and cooked Snow's dog, Pepper, into a chow
mein dish, and then feuded with Big Show in 2000 during the brief
Terry Taylor booking regime by insulting Show's dead father and
even going so far as hijacking the funeral by stealing the coffin while

Show rode on it in a scene out of a surreal black comedy. By the end of 2000, Bossman needed what turned out to be career-ending knee surgery, and he left wrestling to become a trainer in the WWF's developmental division. He expected to return to the WWE at some point and was scheduled for a reunion show with the Midnight Express, but he went to sleep on the couch and was found a few hours later by his wife, dead from a heart attack. It was never revealed if drugs played a part in his death, although he had a painkiller problem and hung with heavy substance users like Hennig and Rude, so it's easy to speculate.

Overall, I've not included another huge group of wrestlers and managers who died in the years before 1997 of drug-related causes. We'd be here all day if I also brought up Art Barr (OD at 28), Buzz Sawyer (OD at 32), Eddie Gilbert (heart attack at 33), Emory Hale (heart attack at 38), Jeep Swenson (heart attack at 40), John Kronus (OD at 38), Larry Cameron (heart attack at 41), The Renegade (suicide at 33), Sherri Martel (OD at 49), The Wall (heart attack at 35), Bertha Faye (OD at 40), and a host of independent wrestlers who did whatever they needed to get to the big dance but never made it.

Hey, here's more numbers to depress you. I went through and charted all the WWF PPV shows from 1986–1996, the peak of the drug era, and counted all the wrestlers on the show and how many of them ended up dead as of this writing. I'm not even counting easy ones like announcers and managers, either, just people who worked matches in the ring on each show. Sorry for the lengthy table here, but it illustrates a point I need to make.

Show Name	Wrestlers on Show	No. Dead	Percentage
Wrestlemania	22	3	13.64
Wrestling Classic	18	4	22.22

Wrestlemania 2	40	7	17.50
Wrestlemania III	38	6	15.79
Survivor Series 87	50	7	14.00
Royal Rumble 88	30	4	13.33
Wrestlemania IV	48	7	14.58
Summerslam 88	28	8	28.57
Survivor Series 88	50	9	18.00
Royal Rumble 89	42	8	19.05
Wrestlemania V	39	8	20.51
Summerslam 89	30	5	16.67
Survivor Series 89	40	8	20.00
Royal Rumble 90	40	8	20.00
Wrestlemania VI	36	10	27.78
Summerslam 90	26	9	34.62
Survivor Series 90	40	8	20.00
Royal Rumble 91	44	9	20.45
Wrestlemania VII	36	9	25.00
Summerslam 91	27	7	25.93
Survivor Series 91	32	6	18.75
Royal Rumble 92	44	7	15.91
Wrestlemania VIII	26	3	11.54
Summerslam 92	22	4	18.18
Survivor Series 92	26	5	19.23
Royal Rumble 93	40	6	15.00
Wrestlemania IX	20	3	15.00
King of the Ring 93	20	4	20.00
Summerslam 93	25	3	12.00
Survivor Series 93	36	4	11.11

Royal Rumble 94	40	4	10.00
Wrestlemania X	20	5	25.00
King of the Ring 94	16	4	25.00
Summerslam 94	16	2	12.50
Survivor Series 94	32	4	12.50
Royal Rumble 95	40	5	12.50
Wrestlemania XI	18	4	22.22
In Your House 1	14	2	14.29
King of the Ring 95	14	2	14.29
In Your House 2	16	4	25.00
In Your House 3	14	4	28.57
Summerslam 95	20	2	10.00
In Your House 4	15	2	13.33
Survivor Series 95	36	7	19.44
In Your House 5	14	2	14.29
Royal Rumble 96	40	4	10.00
In Your House 6	10	3	30.00
Wrestlemania XII	20	4	20.00
In Your House 7	16	3	18.75
In Your House 8	16	2	12.50
King of the Ring 96	20	2	10.00
In Your House 9	18	3	16.67
Summerslam 96	22	4	18.18
In Your House 10	16	2	12.50
In Your House 11	14	2	14.29
Survivor Series 96	38	4	10.53
In Your House 12	14	3	21.43

Looking at this list, the best they ever managed was King of the Ring 96, where a mere 10% of the then-current talent ended up dead ten years later, although only twenty people worked that show. Royal Rumble 94 is slightly more impressive, with forty people on the show and only four of them dead today, but these shows are the exception rather than the rule. Taking the average of these numbers, we see that generally you can expect that when watching a classic WWF PPV, 17.86% of the people on that show are dead. I hope this scares the hell out of everyone else reading this as much as it does me.

Think of it this way: Although the WWE bragged after the Benoit tragedy that only a few people ever died while under contract to them (technically true), upwards of thirty people who have worked for them on a regular basis since the 1980s are now dead. And it's the same with WCW, so it's not like you can point fingers at the individual promotions here. Baseball, for example, has long been a source of ridicule in the media for its steroid problem, but how many baseball players can you name that have died in the last ten years? Anyone? If I went back to the roster of the 1987 Toronto Blue Jays and discovered that 17% of them were dead at a young age, there would be a giant scandal and a federal investigation. And yet wrestling has escaped with a free pass for decades because no one takes it seriously, and this attitude doesn't help. Even scarier, think about what might start happening to players in more "legitimate" sports like baseball and football who have been dabbling in steroids for years without consequence, although taking hits far worse than what wrestlers endure and without the years of experience that wrestlers have in regulating their chemical smorgasbord on a daily basis. Although it's probably too late for the grotesque mortality rate of wrestling to serve as a warning for people who still work in the industry, it may well serve as a wake-up call for sports like baseball and football as to what can happen if they don't get their drug problems under control immediately.

I think the most telling indictment of the WWE is that they now have a standardized "tribute show" they run the night after yet another wrestler is found dead. If it's reached the point that you have a script for the unthinkable occurring, there's a problem.

DRUGS AND WRESTLING

Like most other wrestling fans with more than half a brain (insert whatever joke you want here), I was kind of stunned when the media jumped all over the steroids found in Chris Benoit's house. Sure, I didn't think he'd be dumb enough to leave them for the cops to find, but certainly you'd think that 100 years of wrestling would be long enough for the media to catch on to the fact that (and I hope I'm not going to give anything away here) *wrestlers do steroids*. Quite a lot of them, in fact. Of course, the media was already in a bit of a tizzy about steroids at the time, what with Barry Bonds humiliating baseball by hitting tons of home runs and Floyd Landis winning the Tour de France by nefarious means. But that was just cheating, and the media was just waiting for steroids to kill someone.

Really, it was a strange kind of media circus that resulted, with headlines trumpeting "Roid Rage!" as a reason for the murder-suicide, as if this was somehow a shocking occurrence that hadn't come up in conversation about wrestling beforehand. What, a professional wrestler using steroids? The devil, you say! Fact is, most of us jaded wrestling fans are well aware of the chemical soup that gets poured in the veins of our favorite guys every day, and we choose to live with it because there's quite a double-standard in wrestling. If you look like an overly muscled superman, you get mocked by the fans for being a roided freak, but you get pushed and protected at the same time. However, get off the gas, and the resulting flabby body can get you mocked by the very fans who so vocally criticize your personal drug choices in the first place. It can be a nasty bit of business. Personally, I've always held to the belief that it's their own business when and what they shoot up, so long as it doesn't affect my enjoyment as a fan. Sure, that might sound a little selfish and callous, but that's what the business is built on, and who am I to go against it?

However, recent developments have caused me to have a change of heart. Like others, I have often joked about all the dead wrestlers in recent years, but seeing my childhood heroes' names laid out on the page, dead from heart attacks one after another, kind of kills the humor. I mean, everyone *knows* that wrestlers take drugs of one sort or another, but it's an accepted evil, because we really didn't think anything could happen as a result. But as the Benoit murder-suicide showed, we were wrong. Really, this outcome shouldn't have been a huge surprise, nor is it the first time that drugs and Vince McMahon have been linked in a scandal. It's just the first time that the consequences of what Vince had been denying so strenuously was suddenly made apparent in a very real way. Back in the early days of wrestling, steroids were certainly known about and used, but it wasn't until Vince's sideshow came to town and started rewarding obvious bodybuilder types like "Superstar" Billy Graham (himself a former Stu Hart trainee under his real name of Wayne Coleman) by putting them in the national spotlight that the roided action-figure superman became the norm. Hulk Hogan turned it into the standard by which all other wrestlers' bodies are judged, and the rest, as they say, is history.

But what about steroids themselves?

Back in the '80s, a popular underground bodybuilding magazine called the *Underground Steroid Handbook* contained the following introduction: "We haven't told you horror stories of steroid abuse because we really don't know any."

Boy, sounds downright harmless. And even amidst all the furor over steroid prescriptions and pill-popping, it's relatively simple to order them online and grab a year's supply of Anadrol or whatever suits your fancy—as long as you're a bodybuilder who is legally permitted to use such drugs, wink wink.

Using steroids essentially gives a person extra testosterone to grow muscles. The average male produces between two and ten mg of testosterone a day, but with supplements the body stops making it and soon you get into nasty cycles where you have to replace it just to stay healthy. That's where the side effects like shrunken testes, enlarged breasts (or "bitch tits" in steroid slang), and hypertension ("roid rage") occur. Most serious, and most apropos to the discussion at hand, are problems associated with the heart that steroids cause. Heart attacks are caused by a buildup of cholesterol on the artery walls, which leaves the heart unable to pump blood through the body. Steroids speed up this process and when combined with human growth hormone, the use of which enlarges the heart and makes it work harder to do its normal job, it's a recipe for death every time. The bitch tits, overactive acne, and shrunken testicles are merely minor (and hilarious) side-effects, but the destruction of the heart is the tragic part of the equation.

I chatted with a bodybuilder and long-time user who prefers to remain anonymous, and he gave me a rundown of the most common types of steroids and associated dosages:

—Nandrolone Decanoate, a.k.a.: Deca Durabolin or "Deca" on the street. This is mostly a bulking drug and is highly desired for its quick gains in the way of muscle mass, though water retention makes it unfavorable for contest prep (makes you look bloated). I went from 175lbs to 204lbs in just over 8 weeks on this. Your typical beginner will be on 300mg/week, injected twice per week. Advanced users will go up to 600mg/ week. Use of this drug will shut down natural Testosterone production and result in testicular shrinkage, aka what Benoit had occur to him. His medical problem was most likely a result

of this drug or another DHT-based steroid (dihydrotestos-
terone). This is available only in injectable form.

—Testosterone (available in Suspension, Propionate, Enanthate and Cypionate forms, each having a different period of
activity in the body. Suspension is a daily injection, Prop. is
every other day, Enanthate is twice/week, and Cyp. 1-2 times/
week). Pure testosterone is the basis of every steroid "cycle"
(period of usage and non-usage) and can be for cutting or
bulking. It's usually stacked with other steroids because Test
is hard to use to keep gains for a long time once you're off
of it. 200mg/week up to 800mg/week I've heard of people
using. Side-effects vary from anger problems to acne. Available as injectable only.

—Dianabol, or Methandrostenolone. This is the pill form
of AAS, most commonly seen in high school and college athletes because of its abundance and availability. Because oral
steroids are 17-alpha-alkylated, it takes a tremendous amount
of stress on the liver to process them, resulting in hepatoxi-
city (liver toxic). 20mg/day up to 100mg/day. Available in
liquid or pill form. I've heard of an injectable as well.

—Equipoise. This is a cutting drug mostly used in horses
and cattle. Readily available in Mexico at veterinary stores.
300mg/week to 600mg/week and another DHT-based com-
pound (wrecks the nuts). This is a drug I would say would be
a staple backstage, were I to make an educated guess, for the
purposes of attaining that hard, vein-popping look most wrestlers
have. While it's easy to bulk, it's hard to cut and maintain a low
body fat due to the amount of calories and carbohydrates necessary to consume every day to maintain such size. Drugs like
this encourage fat loss and building of lean body mass.

If you're reading this and thinking "cattle?", you're not alone.
Wrestlers are notorious for shooting up with whatever stupid idea

is trendy at that moment, like monkey hormones in the '80s, for example. And generally they don't care where they come from, as long as it's discreet. Such was the case the first time the WWF nearly got burned by a "doctor" named George Zahorian.

Back in the days when Vince McMahon Sr. ran the WWF TV tapings out of Pennsylvania, Zahorian was retained as a ringside doctor, and was occasionally seen putting bandages on a "wounded" warrior, but he really served no other purpose than supplying the legions of pill-popping WWF wrestlers with their fixes for the week. In 1990 drugs were a hot-button topic in Congress, and the FBI started getting interested in the dealings of Zahorian with regard to a former football coach named William Dunn, who was naming names to avoid jail time. Dunn agreed to wear a wire and meet with Zahorian for a drug buy (a rather large one, at that). The set-up went according to plan and the FBI nailed the good doctor for "prescribing" $25,000 worth of steroids and painkillers to their inside man, and then another bit of information slipped out: the name of "Rowdy" Roddy Piper.

Federal prosecutor Ted Smith went after Zahorian with a passion and, in the process, called Piper and Hulk Hogan to the grand jury to testify, but still no names had been released. That situation changed when Zahorian's attorney decided to cause trouble by mentioning some names:

The use of steroids isn't limited to these wrestlers. They're used throughout the WWF. Wrestlers either use them or they don't participate.

This feeling is backed up by my bodybuilder friend, who adds:

In order to be hired, you must be of a certain physique. In order to have the road schedule and family life a normal person would have, it's impossible to maintain said physique

without proper facilities and genetics. Only certain individu-
als can keep a "buffed out look" without anabolic-androgenic
steroids and most of them probably aren't wasting their time
jumping around in a ring.

Even though this was hardly news to anyone who had been
watching wrestling for more than a couple of years, the press jumped
all over it, specifically focusing on Hulk Hogan. Hulk launched something of a pre-emptive strike against the bad publicity by going on
"Arsenio Hall" and making the following claim:

I trained twenty years, two hours a day to look like I do. I
am not a steroids abuser and I do not use steroids.

Of course, this was shown to be a complete lie, as he later gave
the following testimony under oath during the steroid trials of 1994:

GOVERNMENT: Have you used steroids prior to the WWF?
TERRY B: Yes.
GOVERNMENT: When did you start?
TERRY B: The middle of '76.
GOVERNMENT: What sort?
TERRY B: Injectables and orals. Anabol, decagabril,
    testotosterone. I used deca the most.
GOVERNMENT: Describe steroid use in the WWF back then.
TERRY B: It was common.
GOVERNMENT: Give a percentage.
TERRY B: 75 to 80 percent. Maybe more.*

The government was determined to build a strong case against
Vince McMahon before launching into a full-blown attack on him,

*www.cooldudesandhotbabes.com/hogantrial.html

and this is where their own undoing came in, right from the start. The people who got Zahorian on drug charges were unable to pin anything on the WWF because of jurisdictional problems, and prosecutor Ted Smith had already come to the decision that there wasn't enough evidence in Pennsylvania to nail the WWF to the wall like they had with Zahorian. However, another prosecutor by the name of Sean O'Shea decided to give it a go, using as his "smoking gun" a transaction supposedly made between Zahorian and Hulk Hogan on October 24, 1989, at the Nassau Coliseum where they were running a show. The undoing comes in right away, because there was no WWF show on that night at that venue, which made the government look pretty foolish right off the bat. Still, Vince was panicked and thought that he would end up doing prison time, and the product suffered as a result of his drifting attention.

The first immediate effect was that steroid testing began in earnest, as they tried to put forth a new public image of family-friendly, nonroided freaks. The hammer fell in 1992 with the FBI sniffing around the WWF offices on a daily basis, and then Sid Vicious "failed" a drug test and was fired, followed closely by British Bulldog and Ultimate Warrior. Randy Savage, making his comeback after "retiring" in 1991, shrunk dramatically and took to wearing long tights and a shirt into the ring to disguise his diminished physique. Bret Hart and Shawn Michaels, two guys who probably did take steroids but at least didn't look like it, were pushed to the top and Vince suddenly became a crusader for drug-free morality. Ironically, while all this healthy living was going on in the WWF, Vince pursued his other, even creepier and more homoerotic, passion: The World Bodybuilding Federation. Imagine if you will oiled musclemen posing for the duration of a two-hour pay-per-view event, with the punchline being that Vince actually expected people to *pay* for the privilege of watching it. Even worse, he signed all the bodybuilders to exclusive contracts that meant they could only work for his WBF, which only shot their program once a month. However, steroids don't work that way.

You can't just take them once a month and then go off again; in order to maintain that look, the guys had to essentially sit at home and shoot up, which ensured that a virtual pharmacy passed into the WBF on a daily basis while Vince extolled the virtues of drug testing on his WWF programming. Clearly the government had no clue about the right place to look, because ttheir case was made in front of them but instead they chose to pursue the bogus charges from 1989.

The steroid trial itself was a circus of the first order. The government's main case against Vince was conspiracy and violating FDA law by distributing illegal drugs (i.e., steroids) for purposes of bodybuilding instead of medical reasons. Although the government's main piece of evidence was flawed, they hoped that by calling enough witnesses with personal knowledge of the illegal activities Vince could be trapped into a conviction. And certainly with a maximum of eleven years in prison facing him, Vince was worried enough about the outcome to take the threat seriously. However, he needn't have worried, despite attempts on his part to establish lines of communication in case of prison time (Jerry Jarrett would run the promotion in his stead, for example). O'Shea called Hulk Hogan, Roddy Piper, Big John Studd, Rick Rude, and Kevin "Nailz" Wacholz as his star witnesses, each lacking more credibility than the last. Hogan testified with immunity after jumping to the competition, which left him little motivation to truly cooperate. His memory mysteriously failed him at key points in the testimony that would have linked Vince McMahon to steroid deliveries at Titan Towers. The crowd in attendance was of little help, and treated the proceedings like a wrestling show by booing and cheering the "heels" and "babyfaces" almost on cue. Wrestlers sat in the front row and tried to intimidate witnesses with glares. Rick Rude's testimony sounded bored, and Kevin Wacholz just sounded like a bitter ex-employee out to grind an axe. In short, it was a total disaster for the government and, despite an impassioned closing argument from O'Shea, it took the jury only a day to find Vince not guilty. In the end, the government was unable to prove beyond a shadow of a doubt that Vince had knowingly distributed illegal steroids within his company. The government knew that Zahorian was distributing them, and the WWF admitted that they bought from Zahorian, but Vince's claim all along was that they bought them with a prescription and therefore were doing so under the pretext that it was legal. The prerequisite for conspiracy was thus never met and the government had nothing. But the government was still watching them very closely between 1994 and 1997; a period when, curiously, not many people died of drug-related causes. Almost as if there's a link.

It was really the death of Eddie Guerrero in 2005 that set the whole thing going again. This time, the proposed solution was the Wellness Program, which was a fancy name for renewed drug testing in the wake of an active wrestler on the WWE roster dropping dead of a heart attack. For political reasons there were a few cursory suspensions—like Rob Van Dam and Sabu getting the boot for a minor drug charge related to pot found in their car—but overall everyone on the roster miraculously managed to test clean. Although noted muscleman Chris Masters shrank a few sizes over the period of a month, he gradually increased his mass again once the heat was off, but not before Vince and HHH publicly mocked him on TV for his new body image. And then Chris Benoit died and the finger-pointing started all over again. WWE wrestlers were suddenly all over the media and the Internet complaining about the unfair treatment they were getting. The most awesomely stupid of these complaints came from Ken "Kennedy" Anderson, who posted a lengthy diatribe on his website on the subject, famously ranting that "THINGS ARE MUCH DIFFERENT THAN THEY WERE FIVE OR TEN OR TWENTY YEARS AGO!" (his capital letters, not mine) and that steroid use boils down to "personal choice" rather than the big bad boogeyman of the WWE forcing people to shoot up with monkey hormones to get pushed. He goes on to extol the virtues of the WWE's drug program and how it's comparable to the NFL and NBA drug programs, as though that's anything to be proud of in itself.

This rant is all well and good, but it does raise some rather disturbing questions. If the drug policy that was in place in the WWE is so comprehensive and unbeatable, how did Chris Benoit pass several drug tests in early 2007 although clearly in possession of, and using, large quantities of them? The absurdity here was really highlighted by a statement issued by the WWE after toxicology results came back, which put forth that they were testing for testosterone, not steroids:

> WWE understands that the toxicology reports for Chris Benoit indicate that he tested positive for testosterone and negative for anabolic steroids. On Mr. Benoit's last drug test in April 2007 administered by Aegis Labs, he tested negative for anabolic steroids and for testosterone. Given the toxicology report of GBI released today, it would appear that Mr. Benoit took testosterone sometime after his April 2007 test and the time he died. WWE understands that his dealings with Dr. Astin are currently being investigated, and WWE has no knowledge of whether Dr. Astin prescribed testosterone for Mr. Benoit at some point after the April 2007 tests.
>
> For over 20 years, the WWE has been demonstrating our concern for the well being of our contracted athletes, instituting drug testing in 1987 leading up to our current Wellness Program which began on February 27, 2006, administered by Dr. David L. Black of Aegis Sciences Corporation—one of the world's foremost drug testing authorities.
>
> We believe our Wellness Program is at the very least comparable to those of professional sports and is a program that will benefit WWE Superstars for generations to come.*

*Legal statement issued by the WWE on July 17, 2007

However, no one ever argued that wrestlers *don't* have "freedom of choice" to do what they want with their lives. If someone like Benoit wanted to throw his life away by injecting himself with steroids every day for ten years, that's fine. But that wasn't who he was ultimately hurting. To quote Dave Meltzer, what personal choice did Nancy and Daniel Benoit make? Whose personal choice was it to push Bobby Lashley to the moon before he suffered an injury? Or Batista, another injury-prone muscleman? Or HHH, who has torn his quad muscles on two separate occasions because of alleged overuse of growth hormones? Attacking the people making the accusations is not helping anything. Just because Marc Mero may not have been a "star" in the eyes of the newer generation of workers (and by the way, from 1994 until 1998, he was a huge star) doesn't invalidate the fact that he's faced with a heart valve operation caused by steroids. Kennedy's whole rant is exactly the reason why nothing positive has ever truly happened; the WWF prefers to play the blame game and dismiss the accusers rather than offering a viable solution to the problem. It's ludicrous to say that "We have an extensive drug program and our testosterone levels are blah blah blah" when clearly that drug program let a huge drug user slip right through. In fact, during the initial drug-testing fad of 1992, Vince publicly announced that they had a 100% effective test for HGH, which in fact was a total lie. However, karma proved to be the ultimate victor in the case of Ken Kennedy, as he was suspended in September of 2007 for . . . wait for it . . . being in possession of prescriptions for steroids from a pharmacy that was under investigation by the FBI. Whoops, open mouth, insert foot. Luckily he has not posted any similar discourses on his website since. Even worse was the hypocrisy of William Regal, who got over his drug problems and wrote an autobiography on the subject, but got caught and suspended in the same investigation. That one was pretty disappointing to me as a fan of Regal's.

James Denton of *Fighting Spirit Magazine* offers his own insights on "personal choice":

Personal choice doesn't even enter into it—the mechanism for personal choice is rendered utterly redundant by the hiring policies of WWE, which dictates the schedule and body standard for the entire industry. Steroids and painkillers are absolutely requisite in this business—very few survive the industry without them. That being the case, the "personal choice" is less to do with "Should I put this needle in my arm?" and more to do with "Should I get involved with this business in the first place?" When you consider that God puts certain people on the Earth destined only to do one thing with their lives—whether it's Elvis Presley singing, Michael Jordan playing basketball or Shawn Michaels wrestling—even THAT choice is often made for you. There is no personal choice in wrestling—and there is no personal choice for Nancy Benoit, Daniel Benoit, Debra Marshall, Diana Hart, Debra Argentino or any of the other spouses or relatives who have been casualties of a wrestling lifestyle that they had no "choice" in.

Ultimately the problem lies with the industry itself and its insistence on pushing people based on unreal body types. All the drug problems are just offshoots of that demand. You can test for steroids until everyone in the business is peeing in a cup before each show, but as long as it's still the Bobby Lashleys and Batistas of the world getting the main event push based solely on their big muscles, someone's going to find a way to circumvent the "rules," be it eyedrops in the tested urine or some crazy new form of growth hormone that no one knows how to test. Again, James Denton weighs in:

Fans can be taught to accept whatever is presented, that is not the issue. The issue is, does Vince McMahon—a bodybuilding fanatic and steroid user himself—want to promote a product where the guys do not meet or exceed his own warped standards of physicality? The issue is, does the man who inherits the company, Triple H—who himself is a jakked-up freak with a distorted sense of physique—have what it takes to promote a product that features less-spectacular looking athletes? We know for a fact that Vince cannot help himself. As for Hunter, that remains to be seen, but just looking at him I cannot help but reason that his attitude will be no different to his father-in-law's. British wrestling reached the peak of its popularity (the aforementioned World Of Sport era) with clean bodies and completely natural, non-bodybuilder physiques. It was (presented and accepted as) a sport that was watched and loved by millions and millions of fans every week, with sold out houses everywhere in the country and, at one point, drew a higher rating than the FA Cup soccer final. That was people watching shoot-style, authentic wrestling, not the over-the-top, steroid product of the McMahons. Does wrestling have to go back to that in order to be accepted? Hard to say. But we look at the UFC and see a similar shoot-style, authentic product, with many bodies that are not chemically enhanced—Christ, Chuck Liddell has a beer belly, and he drew 1.1 million buys in December. Fedor Emelianenko is the most dominant fighter in the history of MMA, and he is just a "meat and potatoes" looking guy, not a Mr. Olympia candidate. Fight fans have seen first-hand that great bodies do not equal great talent—the re-education process has already begun in the legitimate combat sports. If the worked combat sport industry is so inclined, it can achieve the same thing.

The UFC is actually a good place to look because they have a strenuous drug program in place and do suspend top-name fighters when they fail those tests. The message sent by the UFC is clear, and in fact owner Dana White put forth a public call for increased government testing of his fighters right after the Benoit tragedy that openly invited scrutiny of his organization to help prevent further tragedies within his own sport. Wrestling, of course, is more about damage control and self-protection, which renders a similar move within the closed ranks of the WWE or TNA a pipe dream at best. Even worse is the attitude of TNA, which, in my opinion, seems willing to hire any castoff from the WWE and push them as their top star no matter what the offense that led to their departure. Kurt Angle had turned into such a basket case by the end of his WWE run in 2005 that even the lax standards of the Wellness Program couldn't excuse his deterioration any longer and the WWE released him . . . right into the waiting arms of TNA, who apparently didn't care that he was a ticking time bomb in need of rehab and not a renewed push. Ditto for Andrew "Test" Martin, who was actually fired *twice* by the WWE for his excessive physique, and even TNA didn't put up with him for more than a few weeks before dumping him. Jeff Hardy was fired from WWE in 2004 after he refused rehab for a very public drug habit—rumored to be crystal meth. TNA hired him without any questions and pushed him as their top star until he was clean enough for the WWE to hire him again. But the worst case had to be Mike "Crash Holly" Lockwood, who was fired from the WWE in a near-suicidal state in 2003 and then picked up by TNA, just because he used to be a name. We know how well that one turned out.

In short, the industry will not change until an agreement is reached on unilateral testing for everyone and would penalize those people who fail the drug tests where it hurts most—their bank accounts. The WWE took a positive step at the end of 2007 by going public with suspensions for ten key figures in the Internet prescription scandal, but more needs to be done. I fear that not much will occur under the watch of Vince McMahon, and probably not under the watch of his successor, HHH, because both are obvious marks for the muscle-man physique. The real change won't come until the WWE has a real competitor, which is not TNA at this point, that's run by people who are willing to take a hardline against drug use and to build their own talent without ex-WWE employees running amok. And wrestlers themselves will not be fully protected until they unionize and demand health care and better working conditions.

Bret Hart is quoted as saying that Vince McMahon treats his promotion like a circus and the performers like animals, and maybe there's something to that. WWE wrestlers are not employees of the company, they are "independent contractors" who must pay their own medical bills and live on the road most of the year. Claims by most current and former WWE wrestlers of "300 dates per year" are pure hokum, as a more realistic number would be 180 dates a year, and that's for some who do every TV taping, house show, and PPV. Like Chris Benoit, for instance. Even so, keep in mind that a football player does no more than twenty dates a year, and football is still considered an incredibly dangerous and taxing sport.

CONCLUSION

I think time and perspective have left Chris Benoit more of a sympathetic figure than he was when he first committed the atrocities of June 2007. Although certainly no one would argue that Benoit was a good person in his last days or that he'll be ascending to heaven with the angels, at least some people can understand that he wasn't in control of his faculties. Again, I spoke with *Fighting Spirit* editor James Denton about the tragedy, and his thoughts sum things up quite well for me.

"I was, of course, completely appalled by what Chris had done. And while I've never attempted to justify what he did, I've always been completely understanding of the horrible, horrible circumstances he was placed under that led to him committing those acts. Thoroughly believe that, whatever else his deeds did or did not make him, they most certainly made him a victim—perhaps the most tragic victim of the wrestling business there has ever been. People are so quick—far, far too quick—to label him as nothing more than 'a monster' or 'a psychopath' or 'a cold-blooded killer'. I believe that is wholeheartedly unfair—this was not a rational man, not a man capable of rational thought. You have to understand the completely warped reality that Chris Benoit existed in, and the severity of the distortion of normality that he suffered. We're talking about a man who subjected himself to twenty years of sustained anabolic steroid and hormone abuse, not to mention recreational drugs and painkillers. Whatever else the pulp media gets right or wrong about steroids and roid rage, the fact is that prolonged manipulation of hormones cannot help but have a profound, pronounced effect on the body and mind, which is only compounded by two decades of recreational drug use and abuse. Then there is the matter of the crippling punishment that was inflicted on his body, much of which was never properly tended to. This is a man who was so possessed of his craft that he wrestled with a broken neck and only considered fusion surgery when it threatened *other people's* health, not his own. Were he not putting anyone else in danger and only damaging his own body, I have no doubt that he would have continued to wrestle until he couldn't move. That speaks volumes about the grip that the business had on him. Consider also the undoubted mental deterioration from concussive symptoms and brain injury, which were an inevitable result of the style he wrestled and the punishment he willingly took— and have side effects of the same disturbed thoughts of inflicting harm that Chris later exhibited. He also lived in the bizarre, hazy world of half-truth, half-kayfabed fiction that wrestling in 2007 had become. Lest we forget just how far the line between reality and storyline was blurred, WWE refused to acknowledge the death of Sherri Martel *because it would undermine the Vince is dead angle.* When wrestling is unable to deal with reality because it interferes with kayfabe, how can we possibly expect anyone so immersed in that business not to be similarly incapable of reconciling one with the other? For Christ's sake, Vince McMahon was blown up in a car accident, which WWE portrayed as real with 'Federal investigations' and press releases, then Sherri Martel died but no acknowledgment was made, then Chris Benoit died with people online theorizing that it was part of the storyline, then Vince *came back from the dead to appear on live TV and announce that he was, in fact, alive, but Chris Benoit was really dead, and it was no angle.* If that doesn't fuck with your perception of reality, nothing will. On top of all this were Chris' domestic problems between two fractured families and the fact that his personal support system completely fell apart with the loss of Eddie Guerrero and

Mike Durham. For all we know, Eddie was the rock that talked him out of committing acts like these in the past—then he died, as a direct result of taking the same shit that Chris was actively pumping into his body. Then Mike, who we know for a fact was often the person who defused violent situations between Chris and Nancy and may have directly prevented such a tragedy happening before, also died from all the stuff he was taking. And when these men died, not only did they make Benoit's entire support system collapse, they left him in a deep, severe depression, which we know leads to suicidal and homicidal tendencies. So what we're dealing with is not a monster, not a cold, calculating murderer, but a victim of the wrestling business who was living and existing in a state of such intense psychosis that, ultimately, it could only end in tragedy—and every cause (with the possible exception of his marital issues) was directly caused by his involvement in the pro wrestling industry."

Even more disturbing than Benoit's death, I think, is the giant list of wrestling deaths that came out after his death. Not that we who follow the business closely haven't heard that list a million times already, but you'd think that wrestlers dropping dead at a rate of ten or more per year would make people stand up and demand action be taken. I don't blame Vince McMahon for people dying under his watch, because I think he's done more than could be asked of the average CEO to ensure that it doesn't happen again. What I blame him for is creating an atmosphere where wrestlers felt the need to look like GI Joe figures come to life in order to retain their position. Although destroying all the competition may have been good for his pocketbook and made sense from a financial standpoint, it also eliminated any sense of competition from the industry and meant that more wrestlers were competing for fewer jobs. And to get those jobs, you had to look like Lex Luger or Hulk Hogan or Rick Rude. Vince tried a drug policy in the '90s, but didn't let it interfere with business. Once WCW came knocking on the back door, the policy was out the window and safety took a backseat. Now you didn't have to just look like an Adonis to get a job, you had to jump off fifteen-foot ladders through tables, climb cages, and take chairs to the head every night. And the fans became as much to blame as anyone by demanding bigger and more spectacular car wrecks out of their wrestlers even though it was obvious that the top names were breaking down by the day. Steve Austin fell apart match after match, HHH tore his quad in the ring on a simple move, and the Smackdown World title has been seemingly cursed since inception thanks to a series of serious injuries that befell anyone unlucky enough to get the title.

There's really only one solution to the problems, and it's a wrestler's union. But that's never going to happen as long as Vince McMahon is alive and I think we all know it. For all he claims to care about his performers, he still doesn't offer health care or benefits. Hell, WWE wrestlers aren't even *employees*, they're "independent contractors," which exempts the WWE from all sorts of legal obligations that even migrant workers get as a result of being employees of a major company. Someone shouldn't have to wait until they nearly die before going to rehab to get help. Guys shouldn't have to wrestle night after night on bad knees, but they do. The grind of a wrestling schedule is awful, even at the greatly reduced numbers that came with the death of the house show era. Back in the '80s, you could expect to do 300 nights a year to fulfill all the dates that the WWF booked. These days, a more realistic number is 120–150, but that's still ridiculous. Baseball players play 162 games a year if they're an iron man and have ample injury-leave privileges and huge leverage in negotiations. Plus they have all winter to recuperate and heal up again before the next season begins. Wrestling is year round, with no breaks. And if you do take a break to heal an injury, someone else steps in and takes your spot, so you don't dare take breaks. Clearly, wrestling needs an "off-season," but that sounds silly just typing it, because wrestling promoters are all unscrupulous bastards who would think nothing of moving in and stealing fans away during off-season.

I, for one, can live without a pay-per-view "event" once a month, or sometimes up to three times a month if TNA is running one and the WWE is running two, and I know I'm not alone. I can also live without three WWE-branded TV shows a week because I used to get by just fine with only one. These days, I get by with none, because the business holds no more love for me now that everyone I cared about has either retired due to injuries or died. I know I'm not alone in that feeling, either, but there's a rule that governs wrestling that says every seven years the audience turns over and a new batch of fans comes in, generally without the benefit of history to teach them what has gone before. It's why good storylines are often recycled, but only after seven years have passed. Sadly, the most frequently repeated story is no angle, and it goes like this:

A wrestler died from heart attack caused by steroid and painkiller abuse at a young age, and no one learned anything from it.

Index

Rizzo, Alex (aka Big Dick Dudley),
162
Road Warrior, The (movie), 135
Road Warriors, 134–42, 168–69
Roberts, Buddy (Dale Hey), 104–5,
125
Roberts, Cheryl, 164–65
Roberts, Jake "The Snake" (Aurelian
Smith, Jr.), 26, 135, 154, 161,
164–65
Rochelle, 60–61
Rock (Dwayne Johnson), 10–11, 98
Rock N Roll Express, 164
Rock N Roll RPMs, 31
Roid rage, 20–22, 123, 138, 177
Roma, Paul (Paul Centopani), 60
Rood, Richard Erwin (aka Ravishing
Rick Rude), 134, 163–67, 170,
184–85
Rose, Randy, 55
Ross, Jim, 55, 98, 131
Rougeau Brothers, 39–40, 69
Rougeau, Jacques, 39–40, 71, 145
Royal Rumble 88, 69, 173
Royal Rumble 89, 69, 173
Royal Rumble 90, 173
Royal Rumble 91, 70, 173
Royal Rumble 92, 173
Royal Rumble 93, 72, 115, 173
Royal Rumble 94, 73, 116, 174, 175
Royal Rumble 95, 46–47, 75, 174
Royal Rumble 96, 76, 174
Royal Rumble 2002, 149
Royal Rumble 2003, 12
Royal Rumble 2004, 12–13
Rude, Ravishing Rick (Richard Erwin
Rood), 134, 163–67, 170, 184–85
Runnels, Dustin (aka Goldust), 65
Runnels, Terri, 65
Russo, Vince, 8–9, 148–49, 153, 171

Sabu (Terry Brunk), 5
Sammartino, Bruno, 28
Santana, Tito (Merced Solis), 38, 68,
146
Sasaki, Kensuke, 140–41
Saturday Night's Main Event, 45,
145–46, 152, 153, 169–70
Saturn, Perry, 8, 125–26
Savage, Randy
and Bret Hart, 68–70
and Curt Hennig, 147
and Dynamite Kid, 35, 38
and Junkyard Dog, 161–62
and Miss Elizabeth, 150–57
Sawyer, Buzz (Bruce Woyan), 172
Sayama, Satoru (aka Tiger Mask), 4,
34
Schiavone, Tony, 171
Seitz, Michael (Michael Hayes),
104–5, 125, 127, 161
Shamrock, Ken (Kenneth Wayne Kil-
patrick), 96, 171
Sharkey, Eddie, 134–35
Sharpe, Ben, 104–5
Sharpe, Mike, 104–5
Shaw, Mike (aka Makhan Singh), 54,
90
Shinzaki, Jinsei (aka Hakushi), 75
Shockmaster (Fred Ottman), 4
Shreve, Larry (aka Abdullah the
Butcher), 28–29
Side effects, of steroids, 179
Simpson, Scott (aka Nikita Koloff),
125, 134, 136–37
Smackdown, 11–13, 130
Smith, Davey Boy (aka The British
Bulldog), 33–52
bar fights of, 47–48
and Bret Hart, 68, 74–75, 78, 82
and Chris Benoit, 3